Geography of Home

Geography of Home

writings on where we live

—⟨⟩—

Akiko Busch

Princeton Architectural Press

PUBLISHED BY
Princeton Architectural Press
37 East 7th Street, New York, NY 10003
212.995.9620

Geography of Home first appeared in an earlier form as a thirteen-part
series in *Metropolis* magazine between March 1993 and May 1994.
Metropolis magazine is published by Bellerophon Publications, Inc.,
61 West 23rd Street, New York, NY 10010

Book design and editing: Therese Kelly
Photographs: Christine Rodin
Special thanks: Eugenia Bell, Bernd-Christian Döll, Jane Garvie,
Caroline Green, Clare Jacobson, Mirjana Javornik, Leslie Ann Kent,
Mark Lamster, Annie Nitschke, Lottchen Schivers, and Sara E. Stemen
of Princeton Architectural Press—Kevin C. Lippert, Publisher

For a free catalog of books published by Princeton Architectural Press,
call 800.722.6657 or visit www.papress.com

LIBRARY OF CONGRESS CATALOGING-IN-PUBLICATION DATA
Busch, Akiko.
        Geography of Home : Writings on Where We Live / Akiko Busch.
            p.   cm.
        ISBN 1-56898-172-4
        1. Room layout (Dwellings) 2. Interior decoration--Human factors.
3. Personal space--Psychological aspects. 4. Interior architecture.   I. Title.
NK2113.B87 1999
728--dc21   98-6588
                                                       CIP

To Brian

Table of Contents

Acknowledgments

Thanks go first and foremost to Susan Szenasy, editor, and Horace Havemeyer III, publisher, of *Metropolis* magazine, where this series of essays first appeared in 1993 and 1994. I am enormously grateful to them for their belief in the value of this project and for their continuing support, both as the magazine series took shape and as it eventually became a book. My thanks are also due to Carl Lehmann-Haupt at *Metropolis* for his encouraging words and dazzling visual layouts. I am also thankful to Linda Bradford whose craft and talent have convinced me that it takes the vegetarian daughter of a minister to make a good copy editor. Likewise, Mara Kurtz's photographs gave color and dimension to the first incarnation of this work. I am indebted also to Susan Wechsler at Fair Street Productions for her enthusiasm and support early on in this project, and for her generous and persistent efforts to bring it into being.

I am grateful as well to Kevin Lippert and Mark Lamster at Princeton Architectural Press for their confidence that these essays might, in fact, make a book; and to Therese Kelly for her thoughtful editing and skillful design that have helped to make them do so. Christine Rodin's spare and elegant photographs speak eloquently to the work and I thank her as well.

Finally, my thanks to my sister Mary for her encouragement, support, and invaluable sense of recall; and to my husband, Brian and to my sons Noel and Luc for being there to live in these rooms with me.

Preface

In the winter of 1992, national news services followed a story about a house that was falling off a hill. For several weeks the image would flash across TV screens and newspaper pages. There it was: a pale yellow modernist house, perched precariously on the edge of San Francisco's Telegraph Hill. As the hill eroded, so did the foundations of the house. At first, chunks of rock fell, then pieces of the house. Finally, the city sent out its public works department with heavy equipment to dismantle the house in a more systematic manner.

The falling house generated many stories; the battle between the architecture and the bedrock was only one of them. Tenants' rights in reclaiming their belongings were also debated, as was the question of who would pay for the demolition: the city or the landlord. When a beautiful house falls apart this way, the image of loss is grand and public, and it stays lodged in the mind.

It stayed lodged in my mind for another reason: I loved that house once. It was where I spent my first night when I moved to San Francisco in 1976. The man who lived there was Charles McCabe, a newspaper columnist. His daughter, Nini, was my close friend, and while her father was away we stayed in his house. It had apartments, and it was built on the edge of a rock. Which meant it was a good place to wake up in the morning. If such a house was possible, you would think that anything is.

I didn't live in the house; I just stayed there for a few nights. But sometimes a brief visit reveals what we mean when we talk about "home." For someone like me who was new in town, the house on its improbable rock represented new possibilities. When a house offers you that, tired phrases such as "the comforts of home" begin to take on an entirely new meaning.

Of course there was more to the yellow house than its picturesque arrogance. You could walk through a small doorway and into the living room, then right out of the house again onto a wide flagstone terrace that seemed to sprawl the world at your feet. The hill dropped away from under you and the stone terrace that floated high above the Embarcadero, the city piers, and the bay. Intersecting with all this beauty was the sense of imminent peril. No easterner could step into such a house, on the edge of such a rock, without thinking of the region's unpredictable fault lines and the very real possibility of the earth opening up. To have the world at your feet and to know that it could all be swallowed up in an instant was a heady lesson for such a small house to offer. I watched it vanish sixteen years later and across 3,000 miles—not in an instant, but in the steady drone of bulldozers and jackhammers. Here is how my friend Nini described the final hours of her father's home: "There are floodlights at the end of the street, and over my shoulder, cops, department of public service guys in orange, huge trucks humming away. It is completely public: cracks and slides are studied, photographed, measured. All day people come along with cameras, wearing sweatshirts, making an outing out of it."

When houses come undone, it is usually through a vague combination of disrepair and memory lapse. The house on Telegraph Hill came apart in a more sudden, abrupt, and physical way. And it cannot, of course, be reconstructed. But when I see something come apart, I wonder how it got put together in the first place—and how that process might be documented.

This collection of writings attempts to do just that. For how we fasten ourselves—our traditions and our values—to the places we live in has all the improbability and vulnerability of the yellow house that was once fastened to its unlikely rock. There are times when the very idea of home seems an impossible proposition. There are other times when our homes express infinite possibilities, when they reflect exactly who we are and what we might be. The idea of this book is to investigate these possibilities—the sure and unsure ground we build on, the foundations, the structure, and the decoration of the places where we live; to take an outing on the varied landscape, the geography of what we call home.

Introduction

My father was a journalist, and much of his work revolved around profiles of the important people of his time, politicians, celebrities, artists. One of the most stringent rules that he established for himself was that he never interview his subject directly. In this talkshow era of uninhibited self-confession, such a stricture seems something between quaintly polite and preposterous. Yet whenever I reread his pieces, it is evident to me how through his conversations with the family and friends, the students, teachers, and colleagues of his subjects, a clear and true portrait invariably emerged. And I believe that while it is not a view that is much in fashion today, news can, and often does, arrive indirectly from the margins of a life; and that the significant facts can often be compiled from the edge of one's life rather than from its center.

In my own work writing about design, I rarely write about people. Instead, I write about the places in which they live, attempting in some way to interview their houses and offices, the gardens they cultivate, the rooms they arrange. By gathering news from the edges in such a way, the presence of places and the people who inhabit them tends to emerge. And in these interviews with rooms, my father's words resonate. I am certain these places reveal something about who we are. I am interested in how places take their shape—why a door has been put just where it has, why a wall is painted a bright canary yellow, why things are the way they are. Eventually, some truth about how we take up space is revealed.

In my own house, that truth—like most other things that are true—is both simple and complicated. My husband and I have an agreement. He was once a contractor, which means he's built many houses for other people. It also means that the one thing he wants to do now is build a house for us, for his own family. It's a project I have little interest in. But we have a marriage, and so we have come to an understanding. He wants to build us a house. Fine. We get the divorce *first*. Then, once the frame is up, the windows are in, and the floors are down, if we're still talking to each other, great. If we're having dinner once a week, better yet. Maybe, eventually, we'll move in together and live in this beautiful house he's built for us.

I don't think this scenario is farfetched. Building houses is right up there with money, sex, and work—all better documented reasons why partnerships dissolve. And I think that's because people disagree so profoundly about what gives them comfort. For me, the comforts of home are inextricably linked with history. The house we live in was built in 1792 and I can't imagine living in a place where no one had ever lived before. My husband's way of finding home is more assertive, less preoccupied with a sense of continuum. As a consequence, in our family the dialog about comfort has to do with whether we find it in inventing our own sense of fit or in distilling it from tradition.

Yet, even with my strong preference for history, not a day goes by when I don't admit that our beautiful two-hundred-year-old house makes little sense for how we live today. The center hall Colonial was not just a building type: it was a pattern for living. Past the front door there is a living room on the right, a parlor on the left, the kitchen and other service areas in back. The bedrooms are upstairs. There is a clear and logical progression to the way the space—passing as it does from public to private realms—has been arranged.

Most homes today express a different logic, one that is more difficult to map. There is no longer a single pattern or cultural definition for comfort. Like so many other things, it's a matter of personal choice. Some friends of mine recently built a house. Midway through construction, they realized that they each held a different notion of comfort. For the woman it had to do with light and space; her ideal home would be built of glass on a mountaintop. Her husband wanted a cave, a nest, a place of warmth and seclusion. He associated home with a sense of physical containment and security. So they found a way to compromise, with an airy, light-filled, open kitchen and living area, and series of more solitary loft spaces to which he could retreat in the peak of the roof.

But in the geography of home, mountains and caves are the least of it. The domestic landscape has shifted in recent years in subtle and significant ways, reflecting the changing structure of the family. In the introduction to his book, *Small Houses for the Next Century* (McGraw-Hill, Inc.: New York, 1995), architect Duo Dickinson observes that the typical family structure today "is fragmenting into a wide variety of households [that include] single parent homes, multigenerational homes, homes that contain offices, homes that harbor empty nesters, homes for unrelated individuals living together as a family, and on and on. . . . Levittown does not fit the 1990s. The idea of small, mass-produced identical houses set row upon row cannot accommodate the extraordinary variety of use patterns homes are put to today." Along with the changing structure of the family, there are growing numbers of people working at home; new attitudes toward privacy, security, and home safety; an aging population; and a nascent respect for the natural environment.

Yet at the same time, nostalgia remains a powerful force in the way we think about home. *The Old-House Journal*, which has over 300,000 readers, sells house plans dating from all periods of American architectural history—Georgian townhouses with elegant brick wall masonry, Carolina folk houses with ample front porches, Italianate cottages with charming arched windows and cornices, seventeenth-century Connecticut saltboxes, and rural Greek revivals with delicate fan windows tucked into the gables. Needless to say, none of these include exercise rooms, home spas, or atriums—just three among the many spaces people seem to yearn for today. The magazine's advertisers offer everything from reproduction Victorian hardware to Amish cookstoves. Never mind that these archaic floor plans and furnishings don't acknowledge any of the economic and social issues that are reshaping our ways of living and working; people still want them. So any definition of home today must consider how new attitudes and values come up against the familiar; how our needs are served by what we know, as well as by what we remember.

That nostalgia plays a part in the way we structure our homes and lives is further confirmed by anecdotal evidence of another trend, dubbed "return migration" by social scientists. For those baby boomers who moved to large urban areas such as New York, Washington, or Los Angeles after college, there is a new appeal, it seems, in returning to the smaller hometowns where they were raised. Never mind that we may use our cell phones, modems, and faxes to stay connected to our reconstructed modern lives. The lower cost of living, the presumed safety of small towns, the greater sense of community, and an extended family—or perhaps simply the memory of an extended family—are all cited as the compelling forces behind this current migration. Nothing confirms social trends in our culture quite so clearly as their being documented by a sitcom. And indeed, "Maggie Winters," "Providence," and "Hyperion Bay" are three such recent shows that send middle-aged professionals back to their rural roots for all the laughs such encounters invariably generate.

A 1994 survey conducted by *Metropolis* magazine reaffirms that many of us do need a little history in our lives. When people were asked what room they would most like to add to their homes, traditional domestic spaces like solariums and music rooms were mentioned as often as spas, lap pools, and home offices. One person wrote evocatively of a mini-pool with a floating office, complete with a sound system, phone, and fax—a kind of combined sanctuary and home office. But a much more significant number said they want a traditional library, a private place to linger over the pages of a book—perhaps a more familiar and reassuring way of getting informed than by surfing the web. Yet the next most popular room on people's wish lists was the exercise room.

When asked to think of their favorite objects, people cited nostalgic, traditional artifacts—a Shaker table, a wicker rocker, a collection of old tins from France, blue glass bottles, an Arts and Crafts side table, a scale model of the Chrysler Building, an old enamel-top kitchen table. It seems that while the floor plan of today's home may change to accommodate new functions, and while we may rely on high-tech appliances in almost every room of the house, the objects of our greatest affections bring a sense of history with them.

We also, it seems, have an affection for morphing space. As citizens of the millennium, we have accepted the idea of a fluid identity as a condition of our times and hold a high regard for personal reinvention. The physical self can be reconstructed at the gym or with more radical "aesthetic surgery" or liposuction, and redecorated with tattoos, body piercing, henna, and other assorted graphics of the human body. Just as we accept morphing identities in people, so too do we find appeal in rooms that mutate effortlessly from one function to another. While many of us use our bedrooms as offices or kitchens as living rooms, it seems we are becoming increasingly creative in how we adapt space. The living room is a place to eat, the dining room or kitchen a place to work, and the bedroom is the library. A hallway with a piano can become a music room, the studio a wine cellar, and, for one especially progressive apartment dweller, the bathtub a conference center.

The proposal that a bathtub might convert to a conference table suggests a new attitude toward privacy. It is no longer necessarily something associated with place. Rather, it may be defined by a change in activity or by a specific time. Often, it seems, privacy is defined not by space, but by a specific activity such as reading, gardening, or taking a walk. Sometimes, it may be associated with a particular time of day, usually late at night after other family members have gone to bed. In crowded cities, where privacy cannot be defined by physical distance, it is often negotiated by controlling sound. Music may be the means to find peace—people turn the phone off and the stereo up. Switching on the answering machine and wearing earplugs or headphones are all ways to limit intrusions.

To get people to think about what home means to them, the survey also asked what room readers most fondly remembered from childhood, and why. The greatest number said the bedroom. "I could hang out under the bed with my cat," wrote one person. The intersection of solitude and fantasy suggested in that statement pretty much sums up the appeal of the bedroom. The kitchen came in a close second, with others writing longingly of the nourishment—both physical and psychological—found there while cooking with their mothers or grandmothers, making meals out of such improbable ingredients as noodles and jam. For all the lures of the electronic hearth, the real hearth continues to have a sustaining appeal in our collective memory. And finally, there are the basement and the garage, by most accounts places that have always been quiet and full of junk—an infallible combination, it seems, to ignite the creative spark in children and adults as well.

It occurs to me that the bedroom, the kitchen, and the basement reflect the three basic realms of home: the private and necessary sanctuary, the place of nourishment and community, the area where things get made. So long as the places we live can accommodate these three very different human activities, it might be called home. When one of my sons first started to color pictures, the house he drew was an imprecise shape, between a circle and a square, with two windows hovering near the top and a door floating somewhere between them. The resemblance of this outline of a simple house to the human face was unmistakable. There is beauty and logic to the way my child confused the contours of a face with the profile of a house. And it occurs to me that this primitive rendering captures the way we imprint ourselves on the places we live.

Just as my son's drawing of a house was also the portrait of a child, I am certain that writing about rooms is a way of writing about people. Words furnish a page, much the way a chair or table may furnish a room. There are times when I think these are parallel processes of assembly. A friend of mine recently returned from a writer's colony outside Edinburgh. The colony was housed inside a grand old stone castle, and every afternoon at four o'clock, the writers would gather in the living room for tea and scones. And they would talk. They would talk not about the essays, plays, poems, and fiction they were writing, nor about their work or their manuscripts or deadlines. What they talked about was how the stone castle was decorated. They would discuss the masonry walls and flowery wallpaper, debate the fabric of the drapes and the stuffed armchairs, and regale one another with the stories about how they were going to go home and redecorate their own homes.

There is something about this anecdote that rings true about the essential connection between arranging words and designing places. Both of these are about finding the logical order of things, about assembling these aggregates of experience in a way that makes sense. A room, like a page, offers us the space to do this. Sometimes that sense of order comes with the way words are arranged on the page. Other times it may come with the way objects have been assembled in a room. Both are ways of finding those arrangements with we which can live.

I am certain that the process of design, very much like the process of writing, is about finding this sense of order to things. Another word for that is fit. And this is the way I try to define design, as having to do with how things fit—

how things fit the hand, how furniture fits the body, how people fit in buildings, and how buildings fit the landscape. What this book sets out to do, then, is look at some of the different ways we find to make things fit. Design, most of all, may be about finding this sense of fit between people, places, and things. And if we think of design as being about fit, we consider not only the physical dimensions, but the moral and social ones as well.

And I would argue that in our increasingly pluralistic, and often chaotic world, finding this sense of fit is ever more important. It may be as simple as the graceful coexistence of technology and nostalgia. And we may need to recognize that there is no necessary dissonance here. My children watch *Terminator* movies on a TV set that is housed in a Shaker-style cabinet. There is a certain postmodern charm to that. But such confusions can also be more jarring. We tend to reject the formal ceremony of the dining room and put the computer on the dining room table, or sort the laundry there. Then, missing the sense of ritual in our lives, we turn to the ceremonies of Native Americans or Tibetan monks. Such incongruities can confuse our lives. But I would argue that they are also the very basis for finding comfort at home. If anything, where we live can be a place that celebrates and thrives on these incongruities that have, in one way or another, been gracefully resolved. If anything, we can find a way to make them fit.

And it goes without saying that this fit is almost always unlikely, idiosyncratic, personal. Where we live can never be landscapes of logic, though they may have logic and precision designed into them. An image of perfect fit that lingers especially clearly in my mind is that of my neighbor, a widow in her late seventies. She lives alone, and beyond her television, has never displayed much interest in modern technology. On a stormy day last winter when I went to visit her, I was expecting her to be sipping hot tea by the fireplace. Instead, she was sitting in her living room, listening to a tape of the ocean. I listened with her to the sound of the surf and the gulls. "I find it so peaceful," she told me.

There is something incredibly modern about this vignette, the way someone who is not of the technological age can use a little technology to find a little comfort. It's a compelling image of a place you might want to live, a landscape where, though you might be hundreds of miles from the ocean, you can find the peace that comes from listening to the waves. Designers and architects often talk about the beauty of multifunctional space, but I can't think of anyone who has achieved this more gracefully than my neighbor who managed to fit the seashore into her little inland bungalow.

Front Door

All my life I've lived in old houses. Except for those years I spent in cities, I have lived in old country houses. Just two of them, in fact: the first was the one I grew up in, and the second the one I acquired as an adult. I bought this house because it was just like the first one, but smaller.

I've been writing about buildings for the past twenty years, asking why they're designed the way they are. But when it came to buying a house with my own family, everything I knew was reduced to the facts and dimensions of a single building type: the New England Colonial farmhouse.

And one of the most important facts that living in a two-hundred-year-old house reminds me of, every day, is how ill-suited these old buildings are to our lives today. The original purposes of the rooms and the way they were laid out rarely conform to our needs. Another fact is that we keep finding ways to make them work. This is true from the time we move in. These adaptations begin at our beautiful front door, which no one ever uses anymore.

While the house itself is a straightforward clapboard farmhouse, the entry porch has slightly higher aspirations, expressed in the Greek Revival style. Three white steps lead up to the small platform with a roof supported by graceful round columns. The ceiling is painted a pale blue and narrow benches frame the front door. A slim transom, with decorative iron scrollwork, and sidelights surround the door, both to bring light into the entryway and to add more ornament to it. All of this spells out the poetry of arrival in a place where no one enters.

We use a side door. The driveway leads around the house to where the kitchen door is. Here is another, bigger porch, where people can leave their shoes and hang their coats. Though less ceremonial than the front door, it is far more practical to come in this way from a car, especially with an armful of groceries. Our beautiful front door and center hall no longer serve the rite of arrival.

A friend of mine went so far as to get rid of the old front door of her house altogether. Her house in Cape Cod is a two-story fifties shingled cabin built into a hill overlooking a cranberry bog. It had a front door with two windows on either side. But almost since the house was built people would pull up to it in their cars, bypass the front door, and walk up a deck that runs along the side of the house to a bigger deck in back, where they'd enter the kitchen through a sliding door. So the family figured that if they got rid of the front door and hall, they could replace it with a large, much-needed closet. And that's what they did. Now, when my friend gives directions to her home, she ends by advising "Just keep driving until you notice the house without a front door."

In that part of myself where I believe that every action in this world is balanced by an act of equal meaning, I am certain there must be someone, somewhere, who is building a Southern Colonial plantation house, which is an architectural style that calls, essentially, for two front doors. The two entrances were a way of solving a venerable traffic problem: Because the side of the house abutting the river was just as likely to bring visitors as was the side abutting the road, necessity and propriety together dictated that both entrances be equally grand and welcoming.

That anyone anywhere is adding an extra front door is wishful thinking certainly. Because when we discuss front doors and why they are where they are, of course, it is not river traffic we are concerned with, but cars. Yet though Americans have been driving up to their houses for decades and entering through backdoors, side doors, kitchen doors, and especially doors through garages, architects keep designing houses with ceremonial front doors that are nowhere near any car or driveway.

There's a middle-income development up the road from where I live in upstate New York. Each of the fourteen houses occupies a half-acre plot and lines up with its neighbors along either side of the access road. Eclectic American is the term that best describes the developer's aesthetic, resulting in a wide, if imprecise, range of historic architectural references. Each house has a two-car garage, and the door that leads from the garage to the interior is used as the major entryway. Despite this significant change in the circulation of the American house—devised to accommodate the car—each house still has a front door. Some are sheltered by gables, others have little steps and porches. There is one with a metal entry porch roof that evokes the Regency style and another that tends toward gingerbread Victorian, though the scale and detailing of these "historic" styles suggests the architectural equivalent of false memory syndrome. Some houses have carefully tended gravel paths leading to their front doors.

These assemblages of curious architectural appendages squarely face each other in their own eccentric conversation.

Like empty lawn chairs after a garden party, these front doors have been abandoned. And I wonder about this. Why do I love my useless front door? And why do these new houses even have front doors at all?

These questions lead to another, more important one, and it occurs to me that the front door may be the first place in the house to ask it, though indoors there are objects, pieces of furniture, whole rooms that continue to repeat it: Isn't there an enormous difference between something that is never used and something that is useless? And if something, like a front door, serves a basic human need for symbolic meanings, isn't that also serving a function? Most car-dependent Americans know that their front door is rarely opened and entered; nevertheless, these doors serve a more symbolic function in that elusive composition of rooms, objects, and ideas we think of as home.

Although it may be unused, the front door continues to appeal to our sense of arrival. Call it the ceremony of coming home. Isak Dinesen richly evokes this experience in *Out of Africa* while describing her life in Kenya in the twenties: "Sometimes Denys would arrive unexpectedly at the house, while I was out in the coffee field or the maize field, bringing new records with him; he would set the gramophone going, and as I came riding back at sunset, the melody streaming towards me in the clear, cool air of the evening would announce his presence to me, as if he had been laughing at me, as he often did."

Here is the idea of homecoming expressed as a sensory experience of music and cool evening air, a sunset ritual. But such rituals have lost much of their meaning in contemporary life. And with this loss we seem to have forgotten the reason we used to have for front doors; yet a memory, which like most memories is at once vague and tenacious, makes us hold onto the idea of them. The architecturally anachronistic front door's main purpose is to be evocative, to remind us of a time when public and private rituals structured people's lives.

We don't shun the front door simply because it tends to be at a distance from the car and the driveway. Most of us stay away from it because it represents a formality for which we have little use. We find greater comfort in informality and choose to make ourselves and our homes accessible through more casual avenues. In suburban America, residents and visitors alike go in and out of houses through garage doors, side doors, kitchen doors. In split-level homes, where the tiny entry hall is poised precariously between upstairs and downstairs, greetings are reduced to awkward and hurried exchanges. There is little place or need in our lives for the ceremonial hallway, designed simply for greeting visitors. Just as we so often use strangers' first names to narrow the distance between ourselves and them, so we enter other people's houses through the unceremonial garage door, arriving in the kitchen, the innermost part of the house. In the poetry of arrival, the garage door is free verse; the front door can be anything from a rhyming couplet to a sonnet.

But there is another reason that the front door isn't used much, and it's that the front door is not an altogether private place. The front door was traditionally designed to present the house to the world at large, to welcome others. It was once the generous, hospitable part of the house. Today as we withdraw from a world which seems increasingly violent and disordered, we tend to view our homes as shelter and retreat; a sense of graciousness offered to the outside world is less relevant to the way we live.

In the rural community where I live, the old-timers still decorate their front doors every season, in a sequence of picturesque signals. In July, flags fly at the door; during the Gulf War bouquets of yellow ribbons streamed from it. In autumn, bunches of corn husks are tied to the doors, and at

Halloween there are paper ghosts and witches. And so the front doors act as a framework to express neighborly sentiments. But for those who have moved here from the city, the Christmas wreath for the door seems enough. Welcoming the world to our door no longer comes naturally. This shift in attitudes is expressed in the world of difference between the airy transom and aged glass panes of my eighteenth-century door and the tiny peephole in the front door of a contemporary city apartment.

The idea that a front door can be a place of gracious convergence between public and private lives calls to mind a couple I know. They live in a converted firehouse in a small Hudson River town. The gigantic openings for the fire trucks had long been replaced with a genuine, people-size front door, which they had painted a bright, but somewhat restrained, barn red. Some years later they decided to repaint it a more vivid, fire engine red. The day they did this, everyone who passed by had something to say about it. So my friend devised a way to register their votes: He painted one side of a stick with the old brick color, the other side with the bright red and held it up each time someone drove or walked by. With this gesture he recognized the fact that the color of his front door was not just his business. Some people voted without discussion, others expressed their opinions, such as "The bright red clashes with your cars." If there is any part of the home that does not belong exclusively to the people who live there, it is the front door. Whether and how we choose to acknowledge this may say something about the degree of comfort and security we feel inside—and outside—our homes.

But knowing this doesn't bring me any closer to using my front door. Nor will I eliminate it altogether and replace it with a closet, or anything else more practical. It will instead remain just where it is to remind me that the spaces in a house are layered for a reason. When you enter a house through the front door, you discover its interiors in a logical progression, passing from public to private realms—front hall, living room, then maybe later, the kitchen. The front door is the first step on this journey of progressive congeniality.

And in our houses, as in our lives, congeniality comes naturally before intimacy. With its white porch and benches, its pale blue ceiling and transom window, my front door will stay just where it is. A small landing where propriety and poetry converge, it will serve perhaps its most important function of all, a brief reminder that there is an interior logic to the way people's houses, like the people themselves, are revealed.

Kitchen

Your mind is a house. And you're just living in the kitchen." This is the way one of my teachers, a painter and printmaker, used to begin his classes. What he was trying to do, I imagine, was to get his students to think of printmaking as more than just the drudgery associated with silkscreening, and, in the process, to use our time in the studio for making deeper inquiries into our psyches.

His words made me laugh, and when I repeated them to my mother, a gourmet cook, she laughed even harder. At the time she was applying gold leaf to a chocolate soufflé. For both of us, the kitchen was the place where, if you're in the right frame of mind, you might think of doing such a thing. And I've never had any reason to think that what happens in a printing studio can be any more sublime than what used to happen in my mother's kitchen.

The experiment with gold leaf was the kind of alchemy practiced regularly in my mother's kitchen—a laboratory outfitted with red Formica counters and fifties-style, blond faux-wood-laminate cabinets. Even to imagine cabinets like this required a leap of faith, but the incongruity of plastic panels posing absurdly as pine planks was exactly the right scenery for this lab. My mother, like most people who know how to cook, understood that what she was doing was science, and that like any other science it required huge leaps of the imagination—at times even acts of faith. In our house, the kitchen was the place where science collaborated regularly and gracefully with creative imagination. And if I believe today that words like gold leaf and red Formica can occupy the same paragraph, it is only because I was made to understand at an early age in my mother's kitchen that life thrives on exactly such unexpected, unlikely, and unpredictable convergences.

The kitchen has been a laboratory from the start. Architect and historian Sigfried Giedion observed in his 1948 book *Mechanization Takes Command* (New York: W. W. Norton & Company), that the history of the kitchen is, in fact, a brief history of heat sources: "The open flame of the hearth, coal within the cast-iron range, gas, and finally electricity followed one another as the heating agents. Their eras were unequal in lengths. For ages, the open flame reigned supreme. During a half century between 1830 and 1880, the cast-iron range became prevalent. Between 1880 and 1930, the gas range won acceptance. Then, in ever rising tempo, began the era of the electric range."

As Giedion points out, the chimney of the early fireplace was the dominant architectural feature of the home, and the hearth was its center until the fifteenth century. At about that time the kitchen became a separate room in the house, though it continued to be used as the central space. The social atmosphere prevalent in contemporary kitchens is evoked by Giedion's description of the seventeenth-century house, in which the kitchen "often served as the burgher dining room, often as the bedroom too, and occasionally as a social chamber. It was a neatly kept place and its rows of coppers became the display pieces that so often glow in the [paintings of the] Dutch little-masters."

The status of the kitchen was reduced to no more than that of a service area during the eighteenth and nineteenth centuries. As the Industrial Revolution progressed, domestic work became women's work and took a backseat to men's work in the factory. Food preparation was relegated to a separate building, partly because it was thought safer to distance the flame of the hearth from the rest of the house. But it was also kept separate because smells emanating from the kitchen were thought to be vulgar and inappropriate for the other, more genteel areas of the house. There may have been a logic to the way households of earlier generations wanted to keep the odors—from such activities as disemboweling sheep—away and out of the living room, but by the Victorian era, a time distinguished by its avoidance of sensory experience, cooking smells of any sort were thought to be inappropriate for the other areas of the house.

In watercolors of nineteenth-century interiors, we rarely see kitchens—whereas bedrooms, drawing rooms, and assorted salons are all amply illustrated. In the rare event that the kitchen was portrayed, it represented a place where the lower classes labored. Ornament tended to be utilitarian, in the form of gleaming copper pots or brightly patterned tableware. But for all the picturesque quality of these accessories, the room was recorded as a humble place of work rather than as one of pleasure.

The image of the kitchen as a laboratory for cooking was reaffirmed by social reformer Catherine Beecher in the mid-nineteenth century. Her efficiency studies determined that the traditional freestanding tables and dressers should be replaced by compact work surfaces with shelves and drawers beneath them. In recognizing that the storage of food and its preparation were two different kinds of work, Beecher also set the ground rules for the modern kitchen, in which different work areas are clearly established. With the proliferation of appliances that mechanized domestic chores—stove, dishwasher, washer/dryer, refrigerator, and a growing number of gadgets—the kitchen became a locus of rationalized labor.

All that has, of course, changed. Today in many houses the kitchen has become the grandest interior, stainless steel theaters where guests congregate to admire gleaming industrial equipment and the culinary feats of the host or hostess. Cooking has come to be seen as a personally rewarding and sophisticated skill, reflecting a rather different view of the realm of the senses. If the Victorians did their best to express revulsion at the scents of the kitchen, today we have come to endorse them fully, as the growing industry of aromatherapy might suggest, often offering the comforting scents of the kitchen as a venue to peace of mind. The aromas of the kitchen have a high market value at the cosmetics counter as well, where coffee, tea, apricots, figs, ginger, nutmeg, vanilla, and other assorted spices all figure as prominently as exotic florals in costly designer perfumes. And when I put my childhood home on the market several years ago, I was advised by one broker to have brownies baking in the oven while prospective buyers wandered through—or, at the very least, she said, have a pot of cider with cinnamon in it simmering on the stove. Such comforting scents, it seems, are now thought to enhance rather than diminish both the charm and market value of a house, sending subliminal messages that "this house is a home."

That we have become a culture that so celebrates sensory experience may also have something to do with our increasing engagement with the electronic realm. The study of design and how things take shape in the physical world often illustrates beautifully and precisely the Newtonian principle that to every action is an opposed equal reaction. So as we learn to maneuver ourselves digitally through the immaterial world in cyberspace exchanges, internet communities, and on-line shopping, it only makes sense that we simultaneously cultivate more physical, tangible experiences that demand we use our abilities to see, smell, hold, and touch in a real and visceral way. And the kitchen, of course, is the ideal place in which to fully indulge our love affair with sensory experience.

But the kitchen's newly regained central position in our houses, and in our imaginations, is due to more than just its ability to arouse and celebrate our senses. That the kitchen has become a larger and more prominent room also signals a shift in American attitudes toward domestic rituals and our reluctance to give them up in the name of modern efficiency. While the Victorian kitchen was an expansive series of spaces dedicated to a pantry, a larder, an icehouse, a scullery, and possibly, in the grander houses, separate facilities for smoking and salting meats, its modern counterpart grew smaller. As processed foods became more widely available, the need for all that space diminished, and kitchens and all their attendant areas shrank. Whereas the design of the kitchen once reflected the science of heat sources, in more recent years it has come to showcase the technology of domestic food processing.

Today the kitchen has again expanded, in part because we have set out to rediscover the space in our homes, and lives, for the rituals of food preparation. And we need the space for the appliances with which to do it. Processed foods, like polyester clothes and plastic tableware, are no longer considered miracles of modern science that help to make people's lives easier, happier, more beautiful. Like the poverty of spirit their inedible counterparts represent, manufactured foods have become a sign of nutritional indigence.

So at a time when every kind of food and drink is available prepackaged and ready to eat, we buy juicers for squeezing fresh oranges, electric coffee grinders to blend our own fresh-roast beans, compact ovens for baking bread, pasta makers to extrude dough kneaded from scratch. Trendy catalogs offer us the latest in fruit and vegetable dryers, along with accessories for freezing and canning. Aside from taking up a lot of room, such appliances are costly, and they often remain unused, serving only as the latest status acquisitions of aspiring high-end households. When processed foods were introduced, they were seen as a luxury that would liberate housewives from unwanted domestic labor. Today's luxury, it seems, is to be able to do the work yourself—albeit with the help of your tools.

Our collection of appliances, neatly lined up on expansive kitchen counters and shelving, suggests that there is something soothing about the rituals of domestic labor. A lawyer I know takes pleasure in baking her own bread. Another friend, a production potter, finds peace in folding the laundry. A surgeon I know begins his day by baking fresh English muffins. While mechanization has surely diminished the drudgery of household chores, it seems that when we are able to choose which chores to do and when to do them, they can give us profound comfort. Perhaps the kitchen is the place in the house where we can find some balance to the acceleration in which we are so invested elsewhere. For every fax machine and speed-dial phone, we

outfit ourselves as well with pasta makers and vegetable dryers, willingly giving ourselves over to lengthy and laborious
rituals of food preparation. Which is not to say electronics
haven't found their niche in the kitchen. We also seem to
find a certain zeitgeist charm in using such appliances as
electronic recipe banks with LCD screens and keyboards to
access the ingredients for such traditional comfort foods as
turkey hash and pot roast.

Indeed, the contemporary kitchen holds further evidence that the work done there is soothing. Many newly
designed kitchens incorporate a desk, home computer, bookshelves—a veritable home office. It is the place bills are
paid, important phone calls made, the business of everyday
life attended to, all of it reinforcing the idea that we find
solace in working in the kitchen—and if we don't find it in
baking a loaf of bread, we'll bring other, equally satisfying
work that needs to be done into the room. Indeed, ever
since Marcel Proust watched his morsel of scalloped
madeleine tea cake dissolve in his tea, inspiring him write
what is widely believed to be the preeminent literary work
of its time, food and intellect no longer require separate
realms.

Johnny Grey, the nephew of legendary chef Elizabeth
David and a kitchen designer and innovator, suggested to me

that the kitchen today is even more of a gathering place than a place of food preparation. "Its primary role is now as a sociable space more than a center for food preparation, a trend that will only accelerate with the increase of pre-cooked and pre-prepared foods. I anticipate study kitchens, kitchens with workshop benches, kitchens without cooktops, kitchens with less that twenty percent of the space devoted to cooking. Kitchens may become living rooms with kitchens attached. A new word would be helpful too, or a qualifier, such as the Great Kitchen, or the Sociable Kitchen."

But even as we equip our kitchens with high-tech appliances and gadgetry, we hold onto older traditions that have shaped this room. Traulsen refrigerators, with double doors in stainless steel or glass, oversize mixers and blenders, chrome backsplashes, and rubber hardware all emphasize a heavy-duty industrial aesthetic that has come into the house through the kitchen. Yet as likely as we are to fill our kitchens with efficient production machinery, we also hold onto the vestiges of old-time kitchens, to cozy symbols of nostalgia. Spatterware plates set the table and antique egg-beaters decorate the walls. For every Sub-Zero refrigerator, there is an antique apothecary chest; for every restaurant-grade mixer, a Shaker box. We want the future in the kitchen, but not at the expense of the past.

The epitome of these conflicting sensibilities may be embodied in the current popularity of the Aga cooker. This industrial-strength, restaurant-grade gas stove offers ultra-efficiency and nostalgia at once; with no thermostat and permanently turned on, the stove has different chambers for slow cooking, and hotter, faster cooking; baking ovens, roasting ovens, and a host of burners all offer different cooking temperatures. Developed initially for use in cool, damp climates, the constant heat of the stove also worked as a central heating system, a factor that makes it less convenient for residents in other climates. No matter; the cooker is still a high-status and much desired appliance.

I wonder how Sigfried Giedion would interpret the new preference for gas over electricity as a heat source. No doubt he would point out that for all the nostalgic appeal of these gas ranges, most contemporary kitchens also come equipped with microwave ovens. He also might point out something else of interest: For all our attraction to these high-end appliances, we also like to hide them. Dishwashers that remain silent and wood-paneled refrigerators that camouflage themselves as cupboards further attest to our conditional love for the industrial hearth.

It seems, then, that no matter how far the kitchen goes in becoming a high-tech laboratory, it also remains the hearth, the landscape of sustenance. And the beauty of the kitchen is that it's one of those rare places where we can have it both ways. As the opposing sensibilities of our appliances and accessories suggest, cooking is a science and an act of love. The kitchen is where chemistry and passion intersect, where conflicting sensibilities coexist.

And that's not surprising, for the kitchen is really all about the possibility of transformation. Here, one thing literally becomes another: calves' brains are translated into *cervelles au beurre noir*, egg whites can be beaten into *soufflé praline*, and sugar can be spun to construct a city of flowers. The kitchen is the place in the house where the ordinary becomes the extraordinary

Magic such as this might be called a miracle anywhere else. But this is the kitchen, a more mundane realm. And although these ordinary transformations may not be the multiplying of loaves and fishes or the chemistry that transmutes water into wine, they may be as close as most of us are likely to get to the feast of Cana. For if we are able to perform small, ordinary miracles in the kitchen day after day after day, possibly these will remind us of the greater marvels that might occur outside this room.

Dining Room

*C*all it an inventory of useless things. After the death of my grandmother, my mother and I set out to catalog the contents of her dining room. There it all was: the sterling silver fish-boning fork, the blown-glass carafes used to rinse wine goblets between courses, a small silver object looking something like a Mexican sombrero that had to do with the disposal of tea leaves. And then there were her household tips, carefully transcribed in her precise longhand: "To properly clean gold leaf, chop up one small onion, dip a cloth in its juice, and rub gently on gold leaf."

And all of it artifacts and information no one will ever need again. Picturesque, evocative, and totally useless. We call ours the age of information, yet what strikes me is not how much new information there is, but how quickly old wisdom becomes irrelevant. How to use a silver fish-boning fork was important to someone once; today, its function and design seem more arcane than a software manual written in pidgin English. This is not the kind of knowledge that will ever travel down the information superhighway.

Today, these antiquated facts and artifacts have become the substance of comedy—metaphors for the small-mindedness and pointless formality of our forebears. Yet the room that contained them persists. The odd thing is that though the utensils have become as meaningless as the rituals that surround them, we insist on holding on to the dining room.

My own old house is full of such pointless features. In addition to our formal front door, we have a formal dining room, which, to begin with, is in the wrong place. The house, like old houses everywhere, has been renovated, with various small additions made over the years. At one point the shed in the backyard became the kitchen, and the big kitchen with its massive fireplace was converted to a dining room. This is the first room in the house. There is no entry hall, no mudroom, just the dining room. What to do with it—how to make it function for our particular needs—was among the first questions my husband and I asked ourselves when we moved in. That was ten years ago and we still haven't done anything about it. The dining room is as it was, and sometimes we even use it for what it was intended. So far as I can tell, this is what most people do, whether their house was built in 1792 or in 1992.

Like the front door we rarely use, the formal dining room continues to figure in the floor plan of most contemporary houses. It's a room filled with tenacity. While the way we divide up the house tends to reflect a growing impatience with formality, the room made specifically for dining remains the anachronism we all love. Our attachment to it dates back to the late eighteenth century, when comfort became an issue in the way domestic interiors were arranged. Whereas previously furniture was lined up stiffly against the walls, it was now regrouped in more congenial configurations—the ensemble of dining table, chairs, rug, and chandelier were placed in the middle of the room. The dining rooms of the wealthy replaced the more ceremonial and stately great rooms of baronial manors.

Once perceived as a less formal alternative to the great room, today's dining room is nevertheless a holdover from an era more formal than our own. This evolution toward a casual lifestyle continues: We are more likely to grab breakfast at the kitchen counter or have pizza in front of the VCR than we are to sit at the dining table for a leisurely meal. Recent research at the Rhode Island School of Design has even pointed to the fact that the most common meal in America today is one of leftovers. And yet we hold on to the big table which, in turn, continues to demand a room of its own. Never mind that the dining table may have a computer on it or often becomes the place to fold the laundry or sort the mail. Its surface bears an invisible imprint that indicates the placement of forks, spoons, knives, napkins, and plates, all of them promising order, civility, and good manners. Setting a formal table has retained its appeal through all the changes that have come into the dining room. This room, a small domain of ritual, though out of sync with the patterns of contemporary life, nevertheless seems to answer some vestigial human need.

When they were very young, my twin sons were the kind of boys who could look at a truly beautiful cloud formation and see in it rifles; they used their toast as semi-automatic weapons and lived in a whirlwind of chaos. But what always astonished me about these two small warriors is how they loved to set the table; they could not seem to get enough of this domestic task. Even they seemed to sense that there was something soothing about the rituals of dining. There was meticulous care in the way one carried a pile of napkins while his brother softly laid out the forks. There was a precision in every move they made. And their behavior seemed to suggest that these simple rituals may be balms to aggression.

That small, domestic rituals can quiet the mayhem of the human spirit has been recognized and institutionalized throughout the ages, and recorded in the history of tableware and table manners. To my mind, the seminal moment of that history occurred in 1669, when Louis XIV decreed the use of rounded knives. At that time, knives had sharp, pointed ends and were as handy in resolving mealtime disputes as they were in carving up a tough hunk of meat. By outlawing such lethal cutlery at the table, the French king was making the reasonable suggestion that his court leave their aggressions elsewhere. Thereafter, knives were designed with blunt, rounded ends, and the knives already produced had their sharp ends rounded. Here was legislation that promoted dining as a social, congenial, even gentle act. It was one of those moments in design history when the connection between the form of an object and social intercourse was clear and precise, when the shape of an object and human behavior took their cues from one another in a clear and beautiful sequence.

By the nineteenth century, tableware's complexity of form was matched only by its eccentricity. Who else but the prosperous and peripatetic Victorians could have come up with the idea that separate forks might be designed for the consumption of oysters, mangoes, lettuce, and fish? Such utensils signaled elaborate and bizarre mealtime rituals. As related by Henry Petroski in *The Evolution of Useful Things* (New York: Alfred A. Knopf, 1993), one wealthy Englishman, whose irritation at constantly being interrupted at the dinner table by servants was matched only by his love of gadgets, went so far as to build a railway to connect the kitchen and pantry to his dining room table. An electric car conveying food and wine would come down the track at the appropriate moment, stopping in front of each guest, circling the table, then making its return voyage to the kitchen. Thus a household ritual was mechanized, reflecting the alienations of the new Industrial Age.

While the invention and eccentricity of Victorian dining rituals may have gone the way of its repressed moral code, we continue to have an appetite for ritual and its various accessories. But it is an appetite full of ambivalence—and with good reason. Believing that the family structure had been shaken by industrialization, reformers of the early twentieth-century Arts and Crafts Movement advocated a return to the hearth and to the safety of the patriarchal home. Straight-backed chairs like those designed by Frank Lloyd Wright were stiffly positioned around the dining table, with the place at the head of the table reserved for Father. Although this was a movement that advocated restoring a sense of humanity through the rituals of everyday life, such a furniture arrangement invariably set out to coerce the human spirit to conform to its own strict biases.

Today, of course, we are more casual about the rituals of the family dinner hour. Dr. Helen Fisher, a research associate in the Department of Anthropology at the American Museum of Natural History in New York, suggests, in fact, that that the hour of the family dinner became rigid and fixed only in recent history with the beginning of the American farming tradition, when farm labor dictated that daily household events be strictly scheduled. And she observes that the more flexible dinner hour most American families observe today is nothing new. "I think we're moving forward to the past, towards a dinner hour that on a daily basis is rather flexible, a coming and going," she says. It is the instinct to dine together and to share the meal, she suggests, that is innate and instinctive in all of us.

But if the hour varies, so too does the ritual itself. On the one hand, we are adept at eating with our fingers. Hamburgers, sandwiches, tacos, pizza. Our diet is filled with foods that can be consumed without utensils. At the same time, we pore over catalogs from Brookstone and The Sharper Image, studying gadgetry whose complexity and specificity is. . . well, Victorian. If we were to give up our cultural biases, would we find a coffee mug warmer or an ergonomically correct spring-loaded ice cream scoop any less exotic than a silver pickle fork or cucumber serving spoon? For all their modern efficiency, such objects, as Sharper Image claims, are "useful products that improve the quality of your life and promote family togetherness." The suggestion that the correct use of domestic accessories and implements might enhance the moral life of the user has, of course, a decidedly Victorian ring to it.

Small wonder, then, that the dining room has remained such a prominent feature on the domestic landscape. Engaging in standard-issue postmodern ambivalence, we do everything we can to edge ritual out of our lives, then rediscover its pleasures. As though to compensate for all the Chinese take-out dinners and fast foods we consume, on those occasions when we dine formally, we do it emphatically. In the upstate New York town where I live, the food served at dinner parties is as likely to be Moroccan, Japanese, Indian, or Thai as it is pot roast. Sit down to dinner at the global village and you may get much more than exotic foods. Our hosts punctiliously observe the proper sequence of courses, and diligently provide the correct tableware. Our appreciation for ritual is heightened at these dinners because we associate it with a sense of novelty and a sense of charm.

While we may be impatient, even dismissive, of our own cultural rituals, we are curiously eager to embrace those that are unfamiliar to us. The postmodern landscape is inhabited by people who believe that ritual is not incultur-ated, but invented. Or if not invented, adopted. This is one of the grander conceits of our times. Ritual, like religion, it seems, doesn't necessarily have to have a connection with cultural heritage; it's just another personal choice.

Some friends of mine recently took up residence in a house built in the sixties. Along with its diagonal siding, severely angled windows, shag rugs, and geometric lighting fixtures was an enormous glass dining room table. Its massive three-quarter-inch glass surface, supported by a sculptural armature of chrome and Plexiglas, was an exquis-ite artifact that documented one of the compelling truths of its time: physical constructions, from Lucite kitchen cabi-nets to cantilevered glass skyscrapers, could appear to float. Yet at the same time, as an exercise in transparence, the glass table from the sixties reflected another truth of its time, a genuine uncertainty, veering on outright rejection, of all its attendant history and rituals. The table had a hesi-tant quality, as though it were somewhat unsure of itself, of its place in the room, in the house, in life. Furniture, like people, can be ambivalent. Together with the glass doors adjacent to it, the essential message of the table—and room—seemed to be its promise to simply glide off into some invisible oblivion.

Setting such a table is almost an act of courage, but it might be done if one recognizes an appetite for order. And certainly the Thanksgiving dinner I had at that glass table was an act of defiance: A luxury of damask and silver and platters heaped with crimson cranberries, green beans, and brilliant orange sweet potato all beautifully repudiated the vague colorless, translucence of the table, transforming it into a place of genuine sufficiency, substance and order. And certainly those are what the dining room serves up most efficiently and why we hold on to this room, almost in spite of ourselves. A small acreage of symmetry and ceremony, it is the place where, just as a radish might be served up as a rose, our own rougher impulses find grace and refinement.

Laundry

Things, like people, can show up in the wrong place at the wrong time. The faltering marriage of a couple I know went beyond reconciliation when an unfamiliar blue handkerchief unexpectedly appeared in the dryer. Although this was a revealing moment in the pair's particular gender relations, such occurrences are routine in the laundry room. And anyone who has ever done a load of wash knows this: If the domestic realm is a metaphor for our cultural values, then the laundry room is the place where relationships between men and women reveal themselves most explicitly, most precisely, and most poetically. Current lore, as well as history, is filled with examples of this.

In the vast country houses of Victorian England, doing the laundry was considered woman's work. And while most families did not actually live on such estates, of course, these rural mansions and manors served as reference points for how the middle class *hoped* to live, and function as a barometer of social values because they express the popular ideals from which our own domestic patterns have evolved. While in a less rigid hierarchy housecleaning and cooking might have been carried out by men as well as women, the wash was women's work alone. And wherever women were found in isolation, there was the potential for rendezvous. Throughout history, the place where laundry gets done—be it by the creek or in a freestanding shed—has been the province of courtship.

To remove its steam and smell from the rest of the house, as well as to provide enough space for drying clothes, the laundry was often placed far from the main building. This meant it tended to be near the stable, where the presence of loitering grooms and stable hands suggested possibilities for romantic interludes to the often willing laundresses. Historian Mark Girouard points out in *Life in the English Country House* (New York: Penguin Books, 1980) that "As far as sexual segregation was concerned, the laundry was the Achilles heel of the Victorian country house." The mistress of one such estate is said to have described the laundry as "nothing but a brothel," adds Christina Hardyment in her book *Home Comfort* (Chicago: Academy Chicago Publishers, 1992).

The mechanization of the laundry did little to diminish its association with romance, and the modern-day laundromat holds out similar promises. From generations of TV commercials, we know, for instance, that this is where the naive bachelor is set straight by the single woman more advanced than he in the enigmas of detergents, bleach, and fabric softeners. To encourage the exercise of the libido while people wait for the spin cycle, the managers of some urban laundromats have been known to outfit these places with potted plants and mini bars.

A man I know, now happily married, reports that doing the laundry has become one of his domestic tasks. He admits that his skill in this area is due not to any enlightened attitude toward housework but to his years of bachelorhood when going to the laundry was synonymous with meeting women. Aside from being better for your health and cheaper than the local saloon, the laundromat was an easier place to pick up and screen potential mates. Just by glancing at a woman's wash, he could discern the relevant facts of her life: The presence of a live-in boyfriend, husband, or children would all be made clear the instant she transferred the contents of the laundry bag into the machine. And if the clothes she unloaded indicated that she was unattached, the next forty-five minutes could be filled up with overtures.

These days, the laundry is no longer the domain of women. As the love story between two men in the eighties film *My Beautiful Laundrette* blossoms, the place gets renovated and transformed. This is about as far as you can get from conventional notions of who does the wash. But while the film challenges discriminations of every kind, it continues to reinforce the assumption that the laundry is a place of romance. In more recent film history, *Dirty Laundry* is a romantic comedy documenting the sexual vagaries and blunders and ensuing marital troubles of a New Jersey dry cleaning king. "Infidelity, Jealousy, Revenge. . . It All Comes Out in the Wash," reads the promotional copy for the movie.

For all the pragmatic reasons the laundromat engenders romance, I wonder if there is something else in the act of washing clothes that arouses the senses, if there's a deeper reason why the laundry serves as a landscape of courtship. I suspect this has something to do with the idea that the laundry is a metaphor for secrets. After all, "airing our dirty linen" is the term we use for being too public with our private lives. A friend who's a smoker has run her own informal survey and found that women who are clandestine smokers often hide their cigarettes in their laundry baskets, and the annals of Alcoholics Anonymous also document that it is a favored place to conceal the gin bottle. Perhaps it is this essential association with privacy that gives the laundry its link with eroticism. Washing one's clothes is at once an intimate and functional act, and there is something provocative about such ambiguity.

This, then, is a room with a story to tell. No surprise, then, that it has established a literary tradition of its own. It seems we have a compulsion to document what we have washed, and the laundry list is a constant in the archives of domestic literature. Hardyman notes that archeologists have turned up lists in Cretan script Linear B and in the hieroglyphs of ancient Egypt. Even the term "laundry list" has become a generic reference for any kind of compulsive itemization. Such tallies, in their details of household minutiae, tell their own stories and work as a roll call for the events of daily life, shorthand for what we do, what we eat, with whom we sleep.

Not all of us, of course, do our wash in public laundromats, and as the labor of laundry moved indoors to private domestic space, its erotic opportunities somewhat diminished. Still, the laundry room remains a realm where our gender relations can be played out. Who does the wash, and where they do it, reflect our attitudes toward sex, work, and time. While urbanites can send out their wash, only those with greater resources—in both city and suburb—are able to give the laundry a room of its own, outfitted with sinks for soaking, shelving for detergents, and tables for sorting and folding clothes. The laundry room, in fact, was not part of the original plan in the march toward modern efficiency. When industrial washing machines were first introduced to the home during the 1920s, advertisements featured them in kitchens, lined up with the other household appliances. To put these machines in a separate room was perceived not as a luxury, but as a step backward.

That the laundry room has again become a desirable fixture of wealthy households speaks to our ambiguous relationship with domestic rituals. In this sense the laundry room is like the kitchen. We do all we can to find appliances that will reduce the time and space needed for household tasks. Yet just as soon as we find the right labor-saving device, we look for ways to recover the rituals we have lost. That a traditional laundry room is coveted by many contemporary homeowners says something of the renewed appeal of these outmoded domestic rituals.

This was certainly true in the house I grew up in during the sixties. In our kitchen we had installed an ambitious innovation that had recently come on the market, a combination washer/dryer (the motion of its inner cylinder both washed and tumbled-dry our clothes). But my mother soon found that the machine's efficiency had been overestimated. When it became clear that the clothes emerging from it were neither clean nor dry, she replaced it with a conventional washing machine.

The question then arose, where to dry the clothes? She promptly strung up a line in the grove of locust trees in the back of the house, and for the following twenty years this was where we dried clothes. On cold or wet and subfreezing days we might use some jerry-rigged drying racks indoors, or the upstairs banister. That the dryer was never replaced was a fact I have long attributed to a misguided sense of family thrift. But there was also something poetic about a string of blue pillowcases, a row of white shirts, or a single linen tablecloth hanging out under the trees. Add to that the fresh scent of line-dried clothes, and I now suspect that there was a different reason why my mother never replaced the dryer in all those years. She liked it better this way.

Today most of us don't have laundry rooms anymore than we have billiards rooms for men or withdrawing rooms for women. Nor do we need them. As we aspire to a more integrated approach to housekeeping, a laundry room seems every bit as archaic as Catherine Beecher's nineteenth-century writings about the domestic sciences. A social reformer, Beecher encouraged women to foster the moral development of their families by creating efficiently run households. And while her views on technology were progressive for their time—she did, in fact, espouse the idea of communal laundries, the services of which might be shared by ten or twelve families—her sexual stereotyping of housework was all too traditional. Too, synthetic fabrics have made it easier to clean clothes; and the idea of spending a lot of time sorting, soaking, bleaching, washing, and ironing them has long been rejected.

So today we fit our washers and dryers into some jerry-built space in the kitchen, basement, or garage. And if these machines do have a room of their own, it tends to be called a "utility room"—a neutral and almost clinical designation that has no gender significance whatsoever. We are as likely to find a toolbox there as a bottle of bleach. It is probably nothing but good sense to welcome the appearance of the utility room in our homes. This often small space is filled with justice, showing us, very specifically, how gender barriers at home may gradually dissolve and how domestic labor might be shared more equitably. That said, I can't help thinking of my mother's clothesline and the random ballet of tablecloths and dresses under the locust trees. That slender piece of rope was about as far from a utility room as you could get. Stretched from tree to tree, it spelled out its own simple calligraphy about the small, impractical, and ever personal gestures that remain essential to the comforts of home.

Closet

ove into an old house, and among the first things
you do is compose two mental lists. One itemizes
all the reasons for your wanting to live there. It enumerates
the house's moments of antique beauty—the wide floorboards, the original plaster walls, the panes of rippled glass
in the twelve-over-twelve mullioned windows. But for every
charming detail, there is also a glaring impracticality; and
these make up your second list. And somewhere on that list
is that there are too few closets.

In my own house, there are two small closets that
might have been added early in this century, both of them
downstairs. The two closets upstairs—fitted under an eave
in the hallway—are even more recent. This is the way it is
with old houses, and anyone who has renovated one knows
this. You have to build more closets right away: in the bedrooms, off the hallways, tucked into a knee wall, anywhere
you possibly can. There is no place to put your stuff in an

old house. Which raises the question—Did our predecessors have fewer possessions, or were they less preoccupied than we are with saving what they had?

Visit America's historic houses from the seventeenth or eighteenth centuries, and you sense that the spareness, the lack of clutter, is what gives them their beauty. There's a row of pegs on the wall for coats, a freestanding wardrobe or a trunk, some open shelving in the kitchen. The inclination to hoard had not yet set in. And what the residents did possess, they kept within sight, within reach. Built-in closets came later.

Ed Chapell, director of architectural restoration at Colonial Williamsburg in Virginia, told me that the absence of closets in eighteenth-century houses is explained, in part, by the fact that clothes hangers had not yet been invented. Hangers, he adds, are attributed to late-nineteenth-century Shaker design. Nevertheless, storage space was provided in the homes of the wealthy: clothes were hung on pegs, or were folded and kept in presses, on shelves, or sometimes in chests. In more modest homes, nails were simply hammered into the wall studs.

The built-in closet was an American invention of the early nineteenth century. It "replaced wardrobes, cupboards, and chests, not only in bedrooms, but also in the kitchen," observes architect and critic Witold Rybczynski in his book *Home: A Short History of an Idea* (New York: Penguin Books, 1987). "The shape and location of the closets is fully resolved and has not been improved on since: a coat closet next to the front door, a broom closet near the kitchen, a linen closet in the upstairs hall, a medicine cabinet in the bathroom."

All of which indicates that housekeeping had come to be regarded as a domestic science, otherwise known as "home economics." As a consequence, storage spaces became precisely defined by their functions. Highly complex shelving systems, containers, closets, and cupboards of all sizes and dimensions were specified for everything from crockery and kitchen appliances to bed linens and clothing. But this system of organization had its opponents. Frank Lloyd Wright, for one, seems to have despised anything associated with the common concerns of mere housekeeping. The architect found closets subversive—"unsanitary boxes wasteful of room," he called them—their practicality derived from the petty female obsession with tidying things up. An indication of Wright's attitude can be read in a speech he delivered in 1894 to the University Guild in Evanston, Illinois: "Housewives erroneously gage convenience by the number and size of dark places in which to pack things out of sight and ventilation. The more closets you have the more you will have to have and, as ordinarily used, they are breeders of disease and poor housekeeping."

Although most architects of the Modern Movement didn't accept Wright's bizarre notion that closets breed disease, they were disinclined to make room for closets and storage space. In part, they were encouraged by socialist tenets, which held that sharing the world's wealth meant fewer material possessions for everyone. They designed multi-family housing made with reinforced concrete and steel framing— building materials that helped eliminate the need for interior load-bearing walls and allowed for expansive and open interiors to be shaped only by well-placed columns or movable partitions. They also put a high value on the "integrity" of a structure, often defining it as exposed frames that revealed the methods of construction. As a consequence, closets— meant to conceal things—were not easily accommodated by the new building techniques or ideals that aimed to reveal processes and materials. Modern American architecture and its Colonial antecedent, though each shaped by entirely different views about possessions, both reflect a sense of austerity through the limited storage spaces they provide.

All of this, of course, has changed in recent years. It may be a cliche to point out that we have become a culture that defines itself as much by what we have as by what we do. Mass production has made it easier and cheaper to own more *things*. And, as we become a more transient society, we tend to define home by the accumulation of possessions as much as by place. Indeed, our appetite for things seems to grow in direct proportion to their availability. And our compulsion to save the things we have has changed the geography of home. Contrary to Rybczynski's claim that the efficiency of the nineteenth-century closet may be hard to improve upon, our growing need for storage has outstripped our closets' capacities. In response, a whole new industry has grown up in America.

Our mania for storage starts at the desktop and blossoms from there with boundless energy. The value of our computers, the most sophisticated filing systems we have, is contingent upon the amount of memory they have. We upgrade them by increasing their digital capacities. The mail-order business thrives on the industry of storage as well, sometimes calling its products "tools for living." The store and catalog, both called Hold Everything, address this need exclusively, offering a dazzling array of things to help you organize all your other *things*—canvas and vinyl bedding bags, revolving accessory hangars, cedar sweater stackers, portable closets, drawer organizers, shelf dividers, recipe boxes, and so on. In other words, you can buy more stuff that will make it look like you have less stuff.

The idea behind these myriad storage units is that they are going to help you organize your life, simplify it even. Common sense might dictate that if it is simplification you're after, buying less might be a more direct route. But the message such catalogs put out is that you can possess forty pairs of shoes and still live simply, just so long as you're also outfitted with the multi-tiered cabinet in which to neatly stack them.

And as for the closets themselves, their insufficiency is made evident by the burgeoning industry of storage unit rentals. Compartments of varying sizes, otherwise known as "self-storage units" or "mini-warehouses," each with its own entrance, are assembled in a huge warehouse. The people who manage these places, like personal trainers and casting directors, are in a line of work that wasn't even imagined fifty years ago. For around fifty dollars a month, they rent you a five-foot-by-ten-foot space in which to stow your stuff. Spend more money, you get more space. Sometimes the units are metal, sometimes they are wood. Some are climate-controlled for more delicate valuables like paintings and grand pianos.

What do people put in them? I ask. Cars, furniture, household appliances, tractors, lawn furniture, books, clothing, and tools are some answers. Who uses this kind of storage? I wonder, and am told: businesses with burgeoning document files and antique dealers who need temporary space to put furniture between sales and auctions, among others. But, as often, they are rented by ordinary people who have run out of space at home. Just about anyone can put just about anything in self-storage.

In rural areas, building supply centers are also thriving on the sale of storage sheds. With their gambrel roofs and double doors, these little buildings resemble scaled-down barns. They are easily assembled from corrugated tin panels or cedar, pine, or plywood, and then installed in backyards. Some have windows, shutters, and window boxes, suggesting the quaint notion that one's possessions might benefit from a view of the outdoors.

A neighbor has installed three of these "barns" next to his driveway. I don't know what he keeps in them, but I know it isn't livestock. The tidy row they form reminds me of the way New England farmhouses were "telescoped," their architecture evolving from the haphazard logic of the household's needs. First the house was built, then a woodshed was added, then came a corncrib, a carriage barn, a main barn, a sheep shed, and a dairy barn—all in a continuous row or an L-shape so that the farmer wouldn't have to go outdoors in the winter to tend to his chores. But in my neighbor's backyard these aggregates of spaces are added periodically to accommodate not people or animals or work, but things.

Many of these little barns also double as playhouses, perhaps indicating that the way we collect and keep our possessions is a kind of play, a way we have of entertaining ourselves. At one outlet for these suburban minibarns I visited recently, I overheard one family debating whether they should buy the six-by-six-foot Econo barn, an octagonal Deluxe gazebo, or a playhouse in the shape of a small ship for their children. These assorted pieces of yard furniture, while not quite interchangeable, seem to serve purposes that can meld into one another.

That storage space has such allure to us suggests a dramatically altered relationship with our possessions, and its my own suspicion that Sigmund Freud pointed us down this path. He was, after all, the one who initiated the industry of memory. The father of psychoanalysis was the first to pin a high value on the personal past, that territory in which the mysteries of identity reside. And so we have grown to appreciate what we can remember—the more of it the better.

"This is a place to put the things that you don't need, but that you can't throw away," states one advertisement for a mini-warehouse storage complex. And it occurs to me that this definition applies to a lot of psychotherapy as well.

In learning to live with our emotional past, we value its physical artifacts as well. The more we personalize our possessions, the more we are able to see ourselves in them. And once we have invested ourselves in the things we own, it's difficult to be rid of them. Which is why I am certain that sentimentality is grossly undervalued. While it is often considered a frivolous luxury, I am certain it is, in the end, one of our more important and genuine emotions. For what is sentimentality after all but the opportunity to put a value on the past without putting a clinical burden on it, a way of attaching worth to personal history with a sense of lightness rather than with inevitable and potent psychological meaning?

But the compulsion to save things extends well beyond our objects of affection. I suspect we have another reason for keeping as much as we can as close at hand as possible. Historian and author Mario Praz observes that at the end of World War II, the word "destroyed" was the most frequently used adjective in Europe, and I wonder if our growing preoccupation with stowing away things is the flip side of our capacity to destroy them and ourselves as well. In

An Illustrated History of Interior Decoration (New York: Thames and Hudson, Inc., 1982), Praz says that in the bombed cities, "wherever you looked, you could see only shattered, ruined buildings, the hollow orbits of windows, and fragments of walls, houses split in two, with the pathetic sight of some still furnished corner, dangling above the rubble, surrounded by ruin: pictures hanging on broken walls, a kitchen with the pots still on the stove. . . ." Yet Praz concludes that in the face of near total calamity, what we do best is continue—instinctively—to build, to furnish, to decorate.

And I reconsider this urge to stockpile, whether it is in our hard drives, automatic revolving tie racks, or walk-in closets. And I reassess the charms of the Econo barns at my local hardware store. With all their pine siding and cedar shingles, their elaborate gingerbread trim, ornamental chimneys, and faux wrought-iron door hinges, these diminutive, prefabricated barns that are being installed in backyards, driveways and gardens everywhere may simply be poignant evidence of our conviction that we can provide for ourselves.

Home Office

With the growing appeal of telecommuting and home-based businesses, one in three Americans now works at home, at least part of the time, notes a recent study. Judging from the many books and articles that advise us on the home office, you'd think the idea was something new. Of course, it's not. A view of this space that I especially like comes from the seventeenth-century Chinese painter, Yun Shou-ping, which portrays a scholar in what today would likely be called a home office.

It is, in fact, a bamboo cottage by a mountain stream. The scholar and his companion can barely be discerned among the willow trees, mountains, and clouds. As in most Chinese landscape paintings, there is a sense of continuum between figure, building, and landscape. There is a fluidity, a congruence between man, work, and nature, and it is clear that the scholar and his fragile bamboo cell are simply small pieces in the larger landscape of the natural world.

And it occurs to me that despite all the recent attention given to the allegedly new phenomenon of working at home, this antiquated view of the work place may have something to offer us.

Everything I know about the home office is contained in a single room from my childhood, when my family moved into an old New England farmhouse. The house itself had been empty for twenty years, as had the barn and the stable. There was a tack room at one end of the stable and this is where my father, a writer, set up his office. It was a space about fifteen-by-twenty feet, paneled in vertical fir-beaded wainscoting stained a smoky brown. And though it had three windows, I remember the room being dark and cool. Dust seemed to creep out of the walls and settle on everything; you could see it hanging in the air as shafts of light streamed in through the old glass. Outside were apple trees and meadows, but they seemed separated from this dusky and remote cell by much more than a pane of glass.

The fact that the room had a previous life made it appropriate for a writer. Its history gave it a flavor, a character that made it a good place to sit, to reflect, and eventually, to write. Many home offices are similarly recycled spaces, and the experts tend to disapprove of them, as though such rooms were inadequate without up-to-the-minute light fixtures, power outlets, and phone lines. But these are just gadgets. My father's room had much more than that; it had a story and a life of its own.

Old planks and cinder blocks composed the bookshelves. My father constructed a desk, using the marble surface lifted from an old Victorian dresser and propping it up on two columns of cinder blocks. Today, such a desk might be regarded as a sculptural and inventive assemblage of recycled materials, but for my father those were just some things he had around to build a sturdy desk. The room was heated by a kerosene stove. And the office chair—a Victorian wingback covered in faded brown velvet and stuffed, most likely, with horsehair—was not what today's industrial designers would call ergonomically correct. But when my father used it, he leaned forward to type and leaned back to think, and the old chair accommodated these two positions with beautiful precision. The office equipment, too, was primitive by today's standards. It consisted of a portable Olivetti typewriter, two green file cabinets, a portable Sony cassette recorder, and a black rotary telephone.

But for the sound of the typewriter, this was a silent room—a place of solitude and meditation. Most of all, it was a place of work.

You could call the place my father worked a home office, but I think the poet Anne Sexton used a more accurate term in calling the place she worked "the room of my life." In a poem by that name, Sexton itemizes the accessories and the terrors of the place she worked, observing that there are "ashtrays to cry into, the suffering brother of the wood walls, the forty-eight keys of the typewriter, each an eyeball that is never shut." How precise the poet's words are, for the rooms we use to do our work come to reflect—inevitably—our lives.

This seems to disturb many designers and consultants of the home office who advance the notion that there is some possibility of keeping out of these places any evidence of our lives, rather than searching out ways to integrate the two. We are advised about the best ways to soundproof the walls, to keep the kids away from the computer, to separate utility services of home and office. And I wonder whether such advice is fundamentally misguided. To my mind, the beauty of the home office is spelled out clearly in its name—it is part of our homes.

While most workplaces necessarily establish rules of behavior and dress codes—implicit or explicit—at home we can give free rein to our idiosyncracies. Which means that home is a place where we are free to find our own ways of doing our jobs, ways that are more reflective of who we really are. People who work at home often devise—consciously or unconsciously—deeply personal rituals, eccentric habits, and uncommon ways to use their time that keep them concentrated on the task at hand, all of these strange ceremonies unavailable to those who work in offices.

In her book, *A Natural History of the Senses* (New York: Vintage Books, 1990), Diane Ackerman observes how various writers throughout history have "courted the muse." She theorizes that even the briefest sensory experience can nurture the creative imagination. And this is the great beauty of working at home: It is a place where we are able to court the muse more ardently, more intensely, more passionately.

Ackerman points out that Katherine Mansfield gardened and Dame Edith Sitwell used to lie in an open coffin before they sat down to write. And Friedrich Schiller kept rotten apples in a bureau; often, when searching for a word, the poet would open the drawer, finding that the pungent bouquet released a new reserve of creative energy. It is said that George Sand went to her desk directly from lovemaking, while Colette found that picking the fleas off her cat was the appropriate prelude to work. More orderly and contained,

Stendhal read sections of French civic code each morning "to acquire the correct tone."

I don't know if management consultants are trained to deal with such information. But it is probably worth thinking about because Ackerman has done more than just compile the eccentric habits of a rarefied occupation. Her observations have a certain relevance at a time when the information we traffic in tends to remove us from sensory experience. Even as we are deluged with ever more information via electronic communications, all our rapid-response appliances seem to isolate us every bit as efficiently as they connect us with one another. Direct experience often seems to have been rendered obsolete by information technology and electronic communications.

There was a time, not long ago, when we learned something useful by doing it. Today, we learn by accessing data on a computer screen. Which is why Ackerman's observations are so relevant: Eccentric rituals or any other activities that return us to sensory experience can enliven and enrich the way we work. My sister, who is a poet, uses her car as a seasonal office. "In the summer, when it's warm," she tells me, "my car is my moveable office. On the first warm day, I load it up with my books, papers, magazines, pens, ink, journals, and mail. I get lemonade and maybe something to eat, and I drive to a hilltop where the view is panoramic. And just having that view is very expansive. And it makes you feel very expansive. I roll down the windows and I can hear all the sounds. And near the place I park is a meadow, and occasionally, the cows will all cluster at my car. It's pretty magnificent. There's no other way to look at it."

But more ordinary rituals can animate home work as well; laundry can be as efficient an accessory to work as cattle or fleas or coffins. One friend of mine who is a lawyer has clear ideas about how she might improve her home office. She is an attorney with two kids, and she often works at home. And when she is writing a brief especially, she seems to end up doing a lot of laundry. She puts a high value on not having to account for the way she uses her time. And she also puts a high value on the seamlessness between her professional and domestic life. So when I asked her what she longed for most in her home office, she thought for a minute, then said, an ergonomic desk chair and a new dryer.

The ease with which she has integrated her legal work with her domestic life also reflects something else—women, possibly, are more accepting in general of home work. A researcher for the furniture company Herman Miller once told me that gender may be an issue in the home office, not necessarily for those people who are self-employed, but for those people who work for their employers at home. In investigating the home office phenomenon, his research team found that there was an enormous difference in acceptance. Men it seems, are less accepting of the value of home work. One of the issues of home work, when you are not self-employed—is how to let management know you're working.

Almost exclusively, men found informal ways to monitor and signal the fact that they were at work, whether it was by recording the moment they picked up voice mail, or logging in the time the computer was turned on. Women generally felt that such logging in was unnecessary, finding it easier to connect the idea of work with home. You might conclude that because women have traditionally worked at home, the transition from house work to information work, because it requires less of an attitudinal shift for women, is less difficult for them. Whereas for men, it is still difficult to associate what you do at home with work.

But for men and women alike, it may be possible to reintegrate episodes of sensory experience through the design of the places in which we work. I'm reminded of a friend who upgraded his home office not by purchasing a new fax machine or adding to the memory of his hard drive, but by installing a skylight. Whereas a fax delivers constant information relevant to the work at hand, the skylight delivers constant light of great variety—from the muted gray of a winter morning to the white glow of a summer afternoon. Possibly, you could say that both the fax and the skylight are about maintaining connections. One to your business associates, the other to the larger world. I suspect that my friend chose the skylight because it best fits the way he works. And because, like the Chinese scholar, he knew that the order of the place had something to do with how it fit into a larger landscape.

The essential ingredient to the home office of another friend is a window to the Hudson River. His immense mahogany desk is positioned in front of a window that looks over the river. It is not a necessarily spectacular view, but the frame of the window is simply full of river—a band of fast-moving water, sometimes gray, other times green. In winter, there may be huge chunks of ice churning on its surface. The only thing unchanging in this view is the indication of a powerful current below the surface. There is something at once soothing and disquieting about it all. Call it a coincidence of tranquility and disturbance—it's as good a backdrop for thinking as you are ever going to find. "This view is home to me," my friend tells me. "As many changes as I go through, or as the house goes through, it remains constant: the line of the river, the cut of the old quarry on the opposite bank. Everything else around it is in flux."

With an increasing number of us working at home, setting up an office away from the corporate building has almost become its own industry. Consultants tell us that the ideal home office is defined by the number of telephone lines we have installed, the type of copier we buy, and how much electrical power is available for a computer that is powerful enough to process all the information we are going to need at our fingertips. But in their litany of necessary electronic paraphernalia, the experts rarely address those questions about how home and work can be integrated in a more sustaining way.

A more compelling and complete sourcebook on the subject might be *The Silent Studio* (New York: W.W. Norton & Company, 1976), a compilation of black-and-white photographs by David Douglas Duncan that documents Pablo Picasso's studio. This is a catalog of a life. In one photograph, varnishes, etching acids, and crayons are accompanied by a set of children's ceramic horsemen. In another, on a table of rough wooden planks rest brushes, paints, a candle, a note from Gertrude Stein. And there's one with Picasso's office chair—a rocker with a crocheted cushion—next to piles of unanswered letters and a child's pinwheel.

There are pages and pages of these vignettes. "Unshaded light bulb typified Picasso's casual life-style regarding home furnishings," reads the caption to one of them. This is not what you would call task lighting, and this is not simply a home office. It is the room of a man's life. There's no contest, as far as I can tell, about the kind of room where the work that really matters gets done.

Library

The Shakers have always irritated me. Not that I don't love the benches, candle stands, wheelbarrows, and chests made by members of this now all-but-extinct American sect. But to my mind, the simplicity of line and the sense of industry expressed in these objects aren't enough. It's no big revelation that beautiful objects can come out of limited circumstances; that's one of life's ordinary truths. But exclude sex and books, as the Shakers did, and you begin to define a starved life.

This is what really bothers me most about the Shakers—they didn't believe much in books. They believed in one book, of course, the Bible, and had occasional use for seed catalogs, almanacs, farm magazines, textbooks on grammar or arithmetic. But at a time when Ralph Waldo Emerson, Nathaniel Hawthorne, Henry David Thoreau, and Herman Melville were consigning the American experience to the written page, the Shakers were putting "hands to work, hearts to God." What you were meant to do with you mind was anyone's guess.

Yet for some reason the allure of this repressive sect remains strong. Photographs of the homes of America's rich and famous published in decorating magazines and books would seem to suggest that the same people who publicly defend pornography and rail against its censorship on First Amendment grounds also manage to harbor a romantic attachment both to the Shakers and to the austere benches, boxes, and sewing stands that emerged a century ago from their cult of alienation. What's a little repression and censorship when you've got elegant straight back chairs, exquisite paint finishes, and a knack for dovetails?

Think of this: a Shaker library. This could be a beautiful thing, a simplicity of shelves and books, a composition of essentials—essential information, essential furniture. Such a thing, of course, doesn't exist. While the Shakers did have tables and the occasional secretary to accommodate their limited but approved reading, they didn't have and didn't believe in a room designed exclusively for books. To my mind, this is a big gap in the history of design, and we are the poorer for it.

The library is a room that contains human wisdom. Call it a room that reflects our relationship with knowledge.

Because knowledge is like anything else—when you love it, you want to do something for it. Sometimes you want to build it a beautiful room, which is exactly what the English did, with steadfast elegance, for centuries.

The private library, as we know it today, probably originated in sixteenth-century England, at a time when members of the landed gentry showed off their social status in the books they owned and read. Their libraries may have included only a handful of books, mostly Greek and Latin classics, and some romances. This limited collection tended to be crammed into a small closet attached to the bedroom occupied by the man of the house; it conveyed the owner's erudition and his moral superiority as a man of letters. Among the largest and most famous libraries of the sixteenth century was that of Sir William More in Surrey. Mark Girouard relates in *Life in the English Country House* (New York: Penguin Books, 1980), that along with Sir More's 275 books, his library contained a full complement of the accessories of knowledge—"maps of the world and of France, England, and Scotland, a painting of Judith, a desk, two chairs, a coffer, a pair of scales, a pair of scissors, pens, seals, compass, a rule, a hammer, a perpetual calendar, a slate to write on, an ink stand, and a counting board."

Two centuries later, the library had grown to occupy a spacious room of its own. As well as accommodating books, it now displayed artifacts of travel such as portraits and classical statues from the Greek and Roman eras, signs that the owner's education had come to include travel to foreign lands. By the mid-nineteenth century, a grand library was integral to the English country house and it often contained musical instruments, in addition to a large number of books. Too, billiards and other parlor games were played there. And so the room began to take on a social role in the domestic landscape, serving as a variation on the drawing room (short for the seventeenth-century "withdrawing room"). As the design of the house came to emphasize comfort and convenience over ceremony, women occasionally ventured into the masculine province of the library, in pursuit of social contact as well as scholarly endeavors of their own.

Today knowledge no longer has a room of its own. What it occupies is cyberspace created by a computer with a hard drive and a modem. And with the growing availability and diminishing costs of laptops, knowledge has become an entirely portable commodity. This change from physical space to electronic space signals one of the ironies of our time: the more information we have, the less room we need to put it in. And with computers becoming accessible to ever more people, increasing numbers of us are involved in the pursuit of knowledge. Although the costs of hardware and software are still out of reach for many, the personal computer is now in more homes than the library ever was. As a result, wealth and class no longer determine to the same degree who gets information and turns it into knowledge.

By their very design, software programs can be seen as equalizers, created to appeal to popular tastes. They can teach you American history or South American geography, the time period and landscape accompanied by appropriate musical scores. When your kids click on an educational program called "Where in Space is Carmen Sandiego," they can learn about space through the moves of a detective pursuing crime in the outer galaxies. As Carmen's promotional copy indicates, the program's database includes geography, mythology, and space science, with the latest NASA images and a musical score to accompany your travels. A book, by comparison, may seem slow and plodding, the printed page outdated and staid when one considers how the "Edutainment" sections of computer marts can provide so much fun and fact simultaneously. Like "infomercials," and "advertorials," "edutainment" is a category of information we have had no use for until recently.

The ultimate home library today is, of course, the Internet, the largest collective computer network in the world, that links some seventy million adult users to an international archive of resources and services on everything from up-to-the-minute political analysis, airline tickets, scientific research, and substance-abuse recovery programs to child rearing. In addition to providing data, the Internet is designed to stimulate dialog, reflecting our assumption that the instant *exchange* of ideas is an essential part of acquiring knowledge.

One of the design tenets for the traditional library, even after it became a place for social gatherings, was that it had to have a door. The pursuit of knowledge was considered a solitary affair to be conducted in a quiet place, behind closed doors. This atmosphere of voluntary intellectual exile was reinforced by the library's dark paneling and heavy curtains. Such seclusion, viewed from the cyber cafes we frequent today, seems a quaint anachronism. As the library was transformed to a home entertainment center, the pursuit of knowledge, whether accompanied by a musical score or not, has become interactive and its acquisition participatory.

But I think there is more than meets the eye in this shift from the solitary study to interactive edutainment. The old English libraries I read about are furnished with polished mahogany cabinets and shelves, worn and comfortable leather sofas, overstuffed and body-hugging armchairs. A patina of age and history attends learning, and it is, I realize, an atmosphere of security and comfort. What has changed the most, it occurs to me, is that we no longer associate comfort with knowledge.

"Bodyworks" is a software program designed to teach kids about the human body, and it is marketed as an "adventure in human anatomy." A course in world history for ten-year-olds promises them they will "Relive 3000 Years of Civilization." And the CD-ROM "Rayman," marketed as the "first action adventure game that's educational too," sets out to teach counting skills and place value along with spelling, phonics, and word recognition. Kids take the role of Rayman, who uses reading and math skills to battle the course "through mindbending landscapes on his way to rescue the magic book of knowledge from evil Mr. Dark."

This spirit of adventure seems to be what we now associate most with learning. Learning is exciting, it is challenging, and sometimes it is exhilarating. But it's no longer comforting. The maps and the atlases, the prints and the telescopes, the rows upon rows of leather-bound volumes with which our ancestors outfitted their libraries— all of these created a sense of comfort. Such were the tools with which we might chart the physical world, and then arrive at some understanding of it. And there was a comfort in that.

But that sense of comfort is absent at our computer terminals. A recent study by social scientists as Carnegie Mellon University, which investigated the social and psychological effects of spending time on line, determined that frequent Internet users experienced a higher level of anxiety and depression than those who were on line less often. Whether they were encountering another persona of the evil Mr. Dark, or simply suffering from the illusion of intimacy forged in cyberspace, isolation and anxiety appeared to be a common byproduct of on-line exchanges. Previously, because it generated social contact, on-line time was assumed to be a healthier activity than simply watching TV passively. In fact, however, the study found the interactive medium, for all the virtual relationships it fostered, also generated feelings of social dislocation not so very different from those felt by constant TV viewers. The study was financed by technology companies such as Intel, AT&T Research, and Hewlett Packard, that were all, understandably, surprised and disappointed at the findings.

Small wonder, then, that the home library is a coveted room. Responses to a 1993 survey by *Metropolis* magazine asserted that the room most people longed for in their homes was a library. At a time when information is increasingly exchanged via electronic services, you might think the library is an eccentric anachronism akin to the billiards room. All the same, we still want one. This abiding desire for a library may simply suggest that people who love to read don't always want to read on their computer screens or to have their reading be an "interactive experience." What they want is to linger over words on the printed page and they want to do this while they're apart from others. And they may also hope for an atmosphere of security and comfort that those older libraries invariably convey.

Though we might describe our PCs as "user friendly," that's not the same as comfortable. This is competence, not comfort. And that we neither look for nor find this same comfort in knowledge may be the fundamental difference between a traditional library space and cyberspace. While our search for knowledge may seem to have changed most dramatically in recent years with the advances of modern communications technology, I wonder if the defining moment didn't, in fact, come earlier. Our quest for knowledge passed a milestone on July 15, 1945, in the desert near Alamogordo, New Mexico, where a group of physicists found the ingredients for nuclear annihilation. Two years after the explosion of the first atomic bomb, Robert Oppenheimer, the director of the project and possibly the original Mr. Dark, said in a lecture at Massachusetts Institute of Technology: "In some sort of crude sense which no vulgarity, no humor, no overstatement can quite extinguish, the physicists have known sin; and this is a knowledge which they cannot lose."

Our forebears, tucked safely away in their libraries, assumed there was a comfort to be found in the knowledge they could put their hands on. In front of our glowing computer screens, we no longer make that assumption.

Front Porch

One of the seasonal rituals in our house is the argument my husband and I have each spring about the front porch. It is the kind of gentle dispute that only people who have known each other for a long time can have. We each know what the other is going to say. So this annual disagreement is almost reassuring; like most rituals, it has its comforts.

During the warm months we use the porch as an outdoor room. It measures about eight feet by thirty feet, with one wall of pale yellow clapboard and another formed by a scruffy pine tree. The floorboards are faded green, the balustrades and trim are white. There is an assortment of old wicker chairs, a sofa, and an old table that you can throw a cloth across.

My husband wants to screen it in. He suggests cutting down the pine tree and glassing the room in, turning it into a conservatory with hanging plants and armchairs and books, a room we might use year round. What he wants to do, in other words, is to bring the porch into the house. But I am happy with it just where it is, confident there's a place for rooms that are defined by time and season, these margins of a house that are used for only a few months each year. I am certain that even the thinnest wire screen would be an unwelcome barrier between indoors and outdoors, one that would distance us from the lengthening twilight, the song of the cicadas, the glow of purple loosestrife in August.

In my house, as in most other houses, the porch resides in a realm of uncertainty. It occupies the ambiguous territory outside the house that might also be called the stoop or the verandah, depending on the style of architecture and the geographic location. In the words of writer Susan Woldenberg, the stoop is a composition of "six to fourteen steps, two rails, and a landing. This device, placed at right angles to the other two unrelenting city surfaces, engenders a third dimension to the street, both architecturally and sociologically, providing an interface between inside and outside, private and public, viewer and viewed" (*Metropolis* magazine, March, 1982).

This third dimension—this interface—has long been a tradition of American architecture, both rural and urban. Halfway inside the house and halfway outside, the very ambiguity of the front porch or stoop has encouraged a variety of interpretations and uses over the years. Most of these have to do with casual interaction among people, indicating that the front porch's social function is as important as its architectural definition.

Porches first became popular in southern states—the shade from their overhangs cooled interior rooms during hot spells and sheltered outdoor gatherings. Regions where the ground is swampy and damp developed the tradition of building second-story porches or "galleries," which wrap around the house and serve as upstairs hallways. Architectural historians suggest that Dutch traders, who must have seen plantation houses with verandahs in the Caribbean, brought the practice of building porches here. Hence the frequent appearance of the porch in Dutch Colonial architecture, even in northern climates where it was hardly necessary to cool the interior of the house.

The stoop, as well, came from the Netherlands, where the main floor of most houses was elevated to keep out periodic floods from the canals. Though the streets of New York rarely suffer such calamities, the city's row houses were built with stoops of varying dimensions. Rather than serving any defined architectural function, these stoops conveyed a feeling of comfortable familiarity to Dutch settlers making their homes on an island they called New Amsterdam. Later, the stoop came to deliver its own social message: The raised front door became the more elegant entryway to the upstairs parlor for wealthy residents, while the door under the stoop was the service entrance to the kitchen.

By the mid-nineteenth century, porches were fully incorporated into American domestic architecture, and remained a prominent part of it for the next hundred years. As families began to enjoy the profits of industrialization, the front porch conveyed the unhurried lifestyle of the leisure class. The industrial production of building parts encouraged the design of ornate houses—with especially fanciful front porches—assembled from manufactured parts: nails, posts, and balustrades. Equally important was the growing tendency to romanticize the natural landscape, even as mechanization and industrialization destroyed much of it. The Arcadian movement, with its emphasis on the pastoral life, was most dramatically expressed in the paintings of the Hudson River School—great light-filled canvases of idealized mountains and valleys showing only a trace of human habitation. The front porch, wherever it faced, seemed put there to encourage this renewed, and somewhat nostalgic, interest in nature.

For a full century, until immediately after World War II, the front porch remained a vital ingredient of American architecture. It was the place people gathered news of the world—an outdoor parlor where gossip and information were treated as one. But as Americans took to their cars, this arena for casual social interaction became obsolete. Soon people were driving past their neighbors' houses too quickly, greetings reduced to a quick wave of the hand or the sound of a horn. And the front porch became less inviting with the exhaust fumes of automobiles and the dust that was stirred up. As the car determined the layout of the suburbs—many new developments were built to be driven through, not to be walked in—the most commonly used building types became Tudor, Spanish, and Colonial, all architectural styles without front porches.

Today news of the world comes from other sources. The frame that was once created by the porch roof overhead and the balustrade below, with columns or pillars on either side has been replaced by the television. Unlike the random formation of gossiping neighbors gathered around the front porch, we get our information from art-directed vignettes electronically relayed into our rooms with faster frames and

more action. As for the porch, it has become a place for con-
templating, rather than for gathering, the news of the world.

With its social function all but obliterated, some front
porches serve private pleasures. In rural areas, where houses
are hidden in the woods, porches still function as gathering
areas, usually for people whose homes are too far off the
road for any passersby to be drawn into casual conversation.
The more public activity on our streets, it seems,
the less we use our porches. While Los Angeles has not set
out to give us a model of what American community
life might aspire to, I was nevertheless taken aback to hear
one architect I know explain his decision to enclose an
open-air, second-story porch in a renovation he was working
on for a house in Los Angeles that combined elements
of Spanish Colonial and Mission architecture. "What, you
think my clients would ever think of using the porch?"
he asked. "These people are not the Beverly Hillbillies, you
know."

While stoop sitting continues to be prominently featured in some TV sitcoms about inner-city life, it is more a
convenient prop than a reflection of urban reality. Although
stoops once served as a neighborhood's outdoor living room,
today the threat of drive-by shootings and the fear of random violence tends to empty them of people. A further

testimony to the retreat indoors is the increased use of wrought-iron fencing and window gates.

In the suburbs, where there are still outdoor gathering areas, these are built as secluded decks and patios in the backs of houses where the outdoors can be enjoyed in familial solitude. Such decks tend to be less expensive to build than covered porches, and in new homes today, many of these are left unbuilt altogether, so that homeowners can take on the construction themselves. Such home improvement projects both lower the base price of the house and allow homeowners to "customize" their houses in hands-on projects that rarely demand advanced carpentry or construction skills.

Where front porches *do* continue to be built, it is often in an effort to return to traditions of both architecture and community life. Consider the presence of front porches in one contemporary housing development and its absence in another. In Seaside, a planned community in the Florida panhandle built during the eighties, the front porch was among the amenities that the architects provided. In an effort to create the intimacy and the flavor of a traditional southern town, the planners developed a building code that specified narrow streets, picket fences, balconies, screened-in rooms, verandahs, wood siding, and pitched roofs. Larger houses along the avenue are required to have full-width, two-story porches—all in an effort to promote a sense of community.

But for all its good intentions, Seaside is, above all, a resort town that begs the question: Can a community be built by people who live there only part-time? Residents apparently delight in talking about the easy social interaction that occurs at Seaside, and they mention the rate at which porch furniture gets worn out. Yet I wonder if this has more to do with the frame of mind we adopt while vacationing than with everyday life and its patterns and demands. While the architecture of the houses at Seaside surely promotes some semblance of neighborliness, I suspect that this casual approach to community has more to do with the laid-back attitude we tend to adopt when we're on leave from our year-round homes.

A prototypical community representing what is being called "new urbanism," Seaside takes both its social and architectural cues from tradition. But by failing to recognize our well entrenched consumer habits—we prefer to shop once a week at sprawling discount outlets rather than every day at more expensive village grocery stores, for example— it neglects inescapable contemporary values that make up our national profile. Another of those is our need to feel secure, and the measures we will take to find that security.

A different sort of building plan documents these current societal values. The gated communities springing up across the United States look more directly to clear and present necessity, not past traditions, for architectural inspiration. Such high-security suburbs, as they are sometimes called, reflect a different view of neighbors and community than that seen from the porches of Seaside. Devised and operated by real estate corporations, these communities have myriad covenants and restrictions to govern everything from the color of the curtains to the right to post signs to the right to put up a basketball hoop in the driveway, or clotheslines in the yard. And whereas once their appeal was mainly to retirees, now young families with small children are increasingly drawn to these neighborhoods. And it seems that their guidelines, though more about protecting real estate values than preserving American traditions of freedom, are appealing to a growing number of Americans who find security and comfort in them.

Walls, rather than porches, are a predominant architectural element in many of these communities. On an excursion to one in Green Valley, Nevada, writer David Guterson documents an environment of insecurity and fear *(Harper's*

Magazine, November, 1992). While at Seaside white picket fences can be painted thirteen different shades of white, the walls that encircle each house at Green Valley are "gray colored, split face concrete masonry units, eight inch by sixteen inch by six inch in size, with a four-inch-high gray, split face, concrete block." Guterson adds that the concrete block is specified to be "laid in a running bond pattern," and that "no openings are allowed from individual back yard lots into adjoining areas." Not surprisingly, the kind of casual social interactions that used to bind communities together are avoided entirely at Green Valley.

The desert has traditionally been a place of self-discovery and revelation. And what such a development in the desert community reveals is a new image of home security. "Warning!" the signs at Green Valley read. "Your neighbors are watching." And perhaps such surveillance, rather than someone who drops by with a bit of news, is what makes a good neighbor these days.

As our homes begin to serve as fortifications, we no longer use the front porch for idle talk and business. Because it occupies that vague space between home and the world at large, the front porch is where we put up the barriers. Alarm systems, walls, and fences have become the "interface between indoors and outdoors" that the front stoop once was, evoking a building model from a point even more remote in our collective past than the Victorian front porch—an electronic version of the medieval moat.

In poor urban areas with a high incidence of violence, residents weave fences of razor ribbon above the iron gates and brick walls that may already separate them from the street. *Razor ribbon*. At once lethal and frivolous, the innate contradiction of the words convey their own poetic cadence. As "white lattice work" or "wisteria vine" once evoked the poetry of the front porch, so does "razor ribbon" describe its contemporary condition.

Maybe not exactly; maybe only in thought rather than actuality. Seaside and Green Valley are probably extreme examples of America's injured community life. Most of us live somewhere between the two, in communities that are influenced by fear and nostalgia, but are governed by neither. At least, I hope that this is so. But I am sure of this: If the worn floorboards and beat-up wicker furniture, the lattice and wisteria of the traditional porch have not been universally replaced by the lethal and graceful curlicues of razor ribbon, their place is being taken by the blinking red light of home alarm systems. The nostalgic beauty of the front porch—a place that stands between home and the world—has been tempered by the harsh echoes of our fears.

Bedroom

S ome friends of mine recently had occasion to build a bed. They were renovating the top floor loft of an 1850 industrial warehouse in lower Manhattan, and when they looked to the ceiling joists, which needed replacement, they saw in the beams the structure for their bed. They dismantled the massive roof beams, then measuring twelve-by-three inches, and took them to a machinist who cut and planed them, then fastened the boards together with six-inch bolts. The final structure, weighing close to four-hundred pounds, was a congruence of material and function: the lumber of the skyline used to support nightly travel to the outer reaches of consciousness.

For all the unique poetry of my friends' experience, it also reflects another trend in contemporary domestic habits. We want the place we sleep to be a place of substance. And so our beds, and bedrooms, are growing. How we Americans take up space has always been an essential part of our cultural profile. Our cars, our homes, our urban skyscrapers, all more spacious than those produced by other industrialized nations, express our cultural mania for bigness. Our appetite for size has apparently followed us into the realm of sleep.

That the place is getting bigger may have something to do with the fact that we are doing more there. Today's bedroom is asked to serve a variety of functions. In city apartments especially, where space is at a premium, we seem to want it all in the bedroom—books, telephone, television, VCR, exercycle. The table next to the bed is often a veritable home office, while the cabinet at the foot of the bed has become a home entertainment center. Add some physical fitness apparatus, and you've got a gym. Indeed, one of the things that's remarkable about the modern bedroom is how a room which really only requires a single piece of furniture has come to accommodate so much more. And I wonder if all this activity in the bedroom isn't flexibility in domestic space gone haywire. There's a fine line between furniture and space that do double duty, and spatial schizophrenia.

That the bedroom should be such a hub of activity is nothing new. Historians of the late seventeenth century tell us, for example, that there used to be very little privacy associated with going to bed. Those who did the household's work slept in a single room, often in the same bed. And those who belonged to the leisure classes used their bedchambers as receiving areas; if they were not actually public gathering places, the bedrooms of the nobility were formal reception rooms. Not until the early eighteenth century did domestic privacy begin to play a part in the way people lived—and slept. Architect and essayist Witold Rybczynski explains the change in attitudes and manners from the seventeenth to the eighteenth century by noting that "The transition from the public, feudal household to the private, family home was under way. The growing sense of domestic intimacy was a human invention as much as any technical device. Indeed, it may have been more important, for it affected not only our physical surroundings but our consciousness as well." (*Home: A Short History of an Idea*, New York: Penguin Books, 1987). As the eighteenth century drew to a close, living space became less crowded, and an increasing concern for health and hygiene further promoted the ideal of individual beds and bedrooms.

Now, though, instead of crowding the room with people, we tend to fill it with things that introduce a host of activities other than sleeping. Not surprisingly, as people do more in the bedroom, they rest less there. Perhaps as a result, more and more doctors are advising insomniacs to take irrelevant activities out of the bedroom. "The bedroom is just for sleeping and for making love," one physician told a sleepless friend of mine. "Don't read there. Don't watch TV there. Don't ride your bicycle there. Don't do *anything* else there." In essence, the doctor was telling my friend to return the bedroom to its natural function as sanctuary. He was also suggesting that trying to do all these things from bed suggests fatigue more than it does flexibility. To put it another way, the doctor was saying that there is a time and place for everything.

But even once you remove all the paraphernalia that seems to find its way into the bedroom, the bed itself keeps getting bigger. Trends in consumer buying indicate that while purchases for twin and double beds have diminished in recent years, sales of king- and queen-size beds have grown. Add to that the appeal of sleigh beds, towering four-poster beds, and massive beds with assorted built-in cabinetry and shelving, all of which resemble architecture more than simply a place to lay one's head. It is comfort we are looking for in all of these deluxe beds. I am told by a representative of the Better Sleep Council that the stress levels of contemporary life are driving us to take refuge in these oversize beds, which are no longer just for sleeping, but for sanctuary and retreat as well.

Consider a bed called "The Big Sleep" designed by Dakota Jackson, a furniture designer and manufacturer in New York. Jackson tells me that in his own bedroom there's the "smallest clock radio that makes the smallest sound," and suggests that when you overload your bedrooms with appliances, "it's no longer about room and space, but about series of functions. And you lose something." Jackson set out instead "to build a world within a room. Not a room within a room, but a world." So he built a bed that he describes as "full-figured, overblown. It looks almost like something is about to burst. It suggests envelopment. I was interested in the ideas of tension and release. The forms are very powerful. There is nothing soft about the head-board or footboard. At the same time, the mattress is large, plump. It suggests a loss of control, a release." And Jackson concludes, "There is something soothing about being over-powered."

Jackson's big bed may be about sanctuary, but so far as I can tell, what he's talking about here is dreams and sex. These are probably more practical considerations when you are designing a bed than the measurements for a VCR cabinet. And as experiences that we tend to put a high value on, dreams and sex are also probably the reason we want such enormous beds. Because while the bedroom may be a place of sanctuary, it is also a place of experience. While other spaces in the house may express something about who we are, the bedroom is the place where we engage in some of our more formative experiences, the landscape of affecting and profound personal revelations.

Though other rooms can certainly accommodate physical and emotional closeness, this is the room intended for physical intimacy. Yet for all its potential for communion, the bedroom can also be a place of isolation. There's no greater solitude than that suffered during sleepless nights, when our closest allies are fear, apprehension, doubt; in counsel with them, our psyches go into exile. This is genuine solitude, and it reaches into our dreams where our unconscious unreels itself.

The bedroom, then, is the province of contradiction. A place that serves intimacy as well as it does isolation, it accommodates the extremes of human experience. Because whether you call it dreams and sex, or solitude and intimacy, these are the experiences that the bedroom accommodates with the most grace, the walls that form both a narrow cloister for the soul and a gateway to a wider sphere of human exchange.

Its no surprise, then, that as our beds are getting bigger, so too are we becoming more inventive at finding ways to accessorize comfort. Manufacturers are adding more layers of upholstery to mattresses to make them more plush, more accommodating. There are mattresses designed for something called "seasonal sleeping,"—silk on one side, cashmere on the other. And there is a growing appeal for mattresses with individual degrees of firmness for two occupants and for those woven with natural fibers. "America is just plain tired," the Better Sleep Council representative tells me. "And because people aren't getting that quantity of sleep they need, they're looking for quality."

Part of that quality is a product of how we accessorize. The abundant bedding catalogs today offer linens disguised as English gardens, southwestern serapes, faux country quilts from the heartland. Blocks of marble, ocean waves, and the forest floor all seem to be accommodating surfaces for sleep and contribute to the extravagant archive of landscapes we might choose from for our nightly sojourn to oblivion.

While these over-embellished linens may record the wide geography of dreams we're after, they also articulate a new definition of comfort. It was not always so synonymous with indulgence. Not so long ago, comfort in the American home had connotations of practicality and convenience. In the mid-nineteenth century, domestic engineer Catherine Beecher advocated narrow sleeping alcoves throughout the house for the very reason that these might save space. More recently, when the modernists turned to bedding, they designed thin, polyfoam mattresses supported by slender plywood frames or tubular metal supports; that such beds might also be stacked, folded into the wall or serve as seating as well were all part of their austere appeal. Even just a generation or two ago, the proliferation of twin beds suggested that there was a certain efficiency, an economy attached to the ritual of sleep.

Today, such economy has been replaced by excess. Outfitting a bedroom, first with these plush mattresses, then with Egyptian cotton sheets and ample goosedown comforters and pillows has become its own domestic industry. And I would argue that all these accessories for sleep serve another purpose too; while they may bring us privacy, rest, and refuge, a place for intimacy as well as the quiet replenishment of dreams, they also graciously accommodate oblivion. This is, after all, furniture designed to facilitate our absence from the conscious world. For a culture that regularly confronts the appeal of mind altering drugs, mindless television, and thrill-seeking sports, is it so surprising that our notion of comfort entails mental absence?

Equating comfort with oblivion is not necessarily as feck-less as it sounds. As citizens of the late twentieth century, we are assured that when we entertain oblivion, we are also nurturing the unconscious, the fertile ground that contains the seeds of our well-being. We recognize our dreams for the heavy load they are, so its only logical that we would try to support them with these oversize scaffoldings. If the bed is the furniture of the unconscious, maybe this lavish sleep equipment is just an effort to give it the space we think it needs, a way of demonstrating hospitality to our psyches.

And so, while these oversized, overstuffed, king-sized mattresses may bear little resemblance to their recent antecedents in the history of bed design, they may be closer associates to an older domestic furnishing: the prayer rug. Designed by mattress technologists, then outfitted in linens representing every landscape imaginable, today's beds promise to convey us across some interior skyline to peace of mind. The very structure of the weave on ancient Turkish prayer rugs was a framework for meditation; here, it is the composition of high-tech foam pads developed by NASA, or a grid of sensitive coil springs that respond to every muscle twitch, that gives us the armature for tranquility and pro-vide, as certainly and effectively as their predecessors, a departure gate for the spirit.

Dressing Room

"All women need two things: A full-length mirror and an ice machine," Frances Lear once told a friend of mine who was then the famous editor's housekeeper. My friend, a poet, found this statement of Lear's memorable for many reasons, not the least being the precise manner with which it combined logic with a sense of frivolity.

Logic and frivolity do not intersect often, but the one place where the two are inseparable is the dressing room. An extreme example might be "The Mermaid's Dressing Room," designed by California decorative artist Nancy Kintish and superstar Bette Midler for a benefit auction. The room began with the imagery of underclothing, logical for a dressing room. It also began with the imagery of deep-sea diving, which in this case was pure frivolity. Specifically, it began with Midler's mermaid costume, a glittering, sequined fishtail and bra. Pale green and blue tulle hung from the ceiling. A neon lamp emitted a low, flickering blue light that had an underwater glow, while bubbles spewed from a bubble machine. But most striking was the dressing table. It resembled a deep-sea artifact, encrusted as it was with shards of Murano glass, ceramic tile, bits of plates, marbles, plastic fish, and seashells. Mirrors, blue glass, cascading rhinestones, faux jewelry glittered everywhere, reflecting fragments of the room back to itself.

The dressing room has always been a place of reflections and a place of extremes. In seventeenth-century France, the master bedrooms in the homes of aristocrats were public suites for receiving guests; thus the dressing room was among several private closets and chambers attached to it. Because these spaces were so private, their designs tended to be eccentric, expressing the whims of their occupants in a much more personal way than the more public receiving rooms did.

Precisely because they were private, these closet-rooms were informal places where "unconventional and even rather daring or crazy forms of decoration could be adapted," explains scholar and curator Peter Thornton in his book *Authentic Decor, The Domestic Interior 1620–1920* (New York: Viking Penguin, 1984). "There were closets entirely decorated with Chinese porcelain vases and dishes, and with walls painted with arabesques dotted with monkeys or scenes from the Italian comedy. Such fanciful ornament would not have been suitable in a state room." Like Bette Midler's efforts to transform a dressing room into an aquarium, these historic interiors represent a kind of psychic deep-sea diving.

In the Victorian era, the implicit sexuality of the bedroom made it off-limits as a public suite. Add to that the inhibitions about the human body, and dressing rooms came to serve as private retreats for husband and wife—both from the world at large and from each other.

For me, the dressing room was the one place where metaphor and fact coincided; where the smoke and mirrors were real. I remember my grandmother's kidney-shaped cherry-wood dressing table stenciled with garlands of roses and peonies, and her vampy, low-slung chaise covered in red silk. There were mirrors everywhere—one above the table, one on the wall, and another, a full-length oval mirror, standing on the floor. The room was always filled with blue smoke. Those were the days in the fifties when women rarely attended to the details of their physical appearance without chain-smoking. Smoke and mirrors were the essential furnishings of the dressing room.

But the smoke and mirrors represent the artifice of that chamber as well, and the idea that a sense of self can be composed through a sequence of small gestures: lipstick, eye shadow, a new hat. The dressing room is the landscape of narcissism, an interior space that is completely about dwelling on the self. But more than simply accommodating personal absurdities, dressing rooms for both women and men were historically furnished with desks or writing tables and functioned much like home offices or studies do today, as a place for personal reflection and study. The dressing room was not only about composing your appearance, but about composing your thoughts; about putting yourself, as well as your attire, in order.

You might imagine that such a chamber of narcissism would become a more—rather than less—prominent feature of domestic design in America, where self-absorption seems to shape the national character. But this has not been the case. Like my grandmother's cigarettes, her dressing room too is a vestige of the past. This cannot be attributed solely to expensive real estate, lack of space, or less inhibited attitudes about the human body. The major source of the dressing room's demise may be that we have come to associate it with *frivolous* self-examination. What Freud told us, of course, is that self-examination is a much more sober and complex exercise. Instead of focusing on the ritual of dressing to get ourselves in order, we know that self-possession is the product of a different kind of self-examination, whether through the general confessions made in group therapy and recovery programs, the more structured investigations of psychoanalysis, the more routine prescriptions of pharmacology, or any selection from the host of other available behavioral or cognitive psychotherapies.

As an antiquated throwback, the dressing room is a reminder of the kind of elitist and indulgent attitudes that no longer fit our image of who we are. But its gradual disappearance from the American home also reflects our changing views of privacy. Today's domestic interiors suggest a new definition of privacy, reflecting new ideas about what we want to keep to ourselves and what we want others to know.

For instance, devoid of walls and doors, the flowing spaces of the open plan popular in modern residential design during the seventies prevented people from feeling separate and apart from the rest of the household. Then, during the eighties, postmodernism put the walls and doors back. And a decade of historic reference has helped us think about how we divide up our spaces, how we turn back to separate rooms. While we may be rediscovering the appeal of privacy, we are redefining those areas for which we need it: we may need less privacy for some things, but we seem to need it more for others.

We lament the loss of privacy that appears to have accompanied the revolution in communications technology; private e-mail can be easily accessed by the companies we work for, and our bank accounts, medical records, and credit card files are all apparently there for the taking by any hacker with access to a keyboard and modem. The growing presence of security cameras is cited as further evidence of the looming presence of Big Brother. Yet there is something that rings hollow about our protestations, because at the same time we have become a society that seems to consider voyeurism essential to entertainment—whether it is in the intimate revelations made on talk show confessions, the soaring ratings of the OJ trial, or the immediate publication of the Starr report. If we cherish privacy, it often seems to be more as an abstract theory than as a value we protect for a civil society.

And certainly, privacy is needed less in the traditionally personal and solitary gestures of self-possession. Once a private, domestic space, the dressing room has been transformed to a small, portable psychic space. Frequently it is transplanted on commuting routes—as anyone who has ever looked around in a traffic jam to see how other drivers are spending their time will attest, these serve as a convenient location for applying blush, eye liner, mascara. And the commuter train I often take is filled with women who attend to their makeup with breathtaking confidence, using an assortment of miniscule mirrors and brushes to decorate their faces while the train hurtles into the city. For others, a simple plate glass display window is the public reflecting pool necessary to compose themselves, while yet others may begin the day by stopping at department store makeup counters to have their face put on each morning, at no charge. While all of these venues to self-possession have a certain brash, arrogant appeal, it also suggests that what was once a series of private gestures has become its own form of public theater. Arranging oneself to face the day can be its own dramatic performance.

In providing a private realm in the domestic interior, the exercise room and the home office may be two of the spaces that have taken the place of the traditional dressing room. But I suspect there is another room that has done the most to eliminate the need for this room. With its sense of deep sanctuary and its flirtation with narcissism, the analyst's office has become the place for rituals of self-contemplation, albeit without a trace of frivolity. Just think of the deep-sea diving imagery presented in Bette Midler's mermaid room, itself a metaphor for plumbing the depths of the unconscious. From the very start, when the chaise longue was introduced in eighteenth-century France, it suggested languor and repose. Since comfort and tranquility are necessary to contemplate one's past, thus it was that the traditional reclining chair became the analytical couch.

For years, my grandmother's dressing room furniture has been stored in an old barn in upstate New York. Recently, it found a second life. A psychiatrist I know was looking to refurnish her office, and I mentioned the stenciled writing table to her. Together, we dragged it out of storage. It turned out to be exactly what she had in mind. When she saw the old chaise, she thought that, too, would fit her office well. So my grandmother's dressing room was recreated as an analyst's office. There are no mirrors, perhaps the most important ingredient of any dressing room, but that role, as I understand it, is often served by the analyst.

This makes me think that the world is governed by an interior logic and justice of its own. Here was one of those moments in which the events of daily life and metaphor intersect precisely and perfectly. The table and chaise will once again furnish a room that is a place of reflection and a place of extremes. And in its second life, as it did in its first, this room will serve as a sanctuary. I can't begin to guess the kinds of conversations that will take place there, or what interior revelations will occur. But I am sure that, one way or another, they will be about facing the day.

Bathroom

A surgeon I know uses the shower as a place to prepare for performing operations. "I very often go over the whole operation in my mind in the shower," he told me. "Like the Olympic athlete who reviews every step of the race before he runs it, I go over each step of the procedure." Anecdotal evidence suggests he's not alone. The creative process often seems to begin in the shower, and you can't deny that there is something extraordinary, even magical about this little capsule that drives people to deep thought, and as likely, song. There's been a lot of talk lately about how technology is changing both the way people communicate and the way they string their ideas together in the first place. But in tracking the imprecise paths of the way people get their ideas, I'm more interested in what it is about taking a shower that seems so naturally to engender deep thought.

And then there's the reading. Everyone, it seems, likes to read in the bathroom. We know this. One of the best home renovations I've heard about in awhile was an inspired conversion of a very small powder room. As a gift to her husband, a woman commissioned a series of four walnut cases, moisture-proofed and glazed on either side, to be installed on the wall next to the toilet. Encased in the shelves are his collection of antique illuminated manuscripts and leather-bound volumes. The only other furnishings in the room are a marble sink, a mirror with a gilt frame, and a small chandelier.

For all its apparent eccentricity, this renovation reveals some straight thinking because it recognizes something basic about the room—people use it for reading. Whirlpools, saunas, Jacuzzis, and home spa equipment—the problem with all of these is that they get used only rarely. Architects talk about clients who ask for these various amenities, hoping that the fixtures will help them relax. But so frenzied are their clients' lives, these architects tell me, they don't find the time to use the very household appliances designed for lavish relaxation. Ordinary logic might suggest that when you start to think you need mechanical equipment to help you relax, you're in a state of confusion. There is more honesty in the beautiful set of bookshelves.

It's a small space, but solitude doesn't ask for much. The bathroom—this outpost of privacy—is the only place in the house where we are justified in being alone. From my own informal survey, I know that new mothers, unaccustomed to the constant demands of their infants, put a high premium on being able to lock themselves in the bathroom for long periods of time the instant someone is available to watch the baby. Which may be why the contemporary bathroom keeps getting bigger, almost tripling in size in the past decade, and in the process becoming more luxurious and better equipped than ever before. In decorating magazines, you see pictures of bathrooms with armchairs and tables, exercycles, walk-in closets—the bathroom is often shown as if it were a living room, an exercise room, a dressing room. At the high end are master suites with separate bathrooms for husband and wife, all of which suggests that we are all looking for a piece of privacy in our lives, and that the bath is often the only place we can find it. Once we do find it, we make the most of it.

The irony, of course, is that in Western civilization the bath was traditionally a social place, and the regeneration that comes with bathing a shared activity. The earliest institutionalized baths we know of were in ancient Greece, where ablutions were conducted in the gymnasium—the arena for both physical and intellectual development. The Romans, who developed the aqueduct, also found a way to heat water; their elaborate bathing rituals took place in rooms of varying temperatures that also served as gymnasia, libraries, and gathering places. In Islamic countries, bathing was less about physical or mental exercise and had more to do with repose. Elsewhere in the world today, bathing remains a social activity. In Japan, it is a communal ritual that strengthens family ties. The Finns take saunas, and the icy plunges that follow the dry heat, together. Turkish steam baths are places for women to gather, gossip, and exchange advice. But we Americans cling to our privacy.

Even when we adapt the bathing rituals of other cultures, we put our own cultural spin on them. In trying to adopt the customs of the Japanese hot tub, for example, we have managed to transform it from a soothing family ritual to a place for social or romantic exchange—with all the innate tensions that invariably attend such gatherings. But a comedy of manners inevitably ensues when the bathing rituals of one culture are grafted onto another. My father traveled as a journalist to Saudi Arabia during the forties and was a guest at the palace of King Ibn Saud. The bathroom in the guest quarters was lavish, the tub enormous, and the faucets and fixtures plated in gold. Yet every time he turned on the water, he heard a rustle of activity overhead and, often, giggles. It didn't take him long to discover a tiny peephole in the ceiling, through which several small boys were observing his every move and then pouring buckets of hot or cold water into the appropriate pipe. The opulent fixtures were a mere show and the plumbing was rudimentary—which made his privacy nonexistent.

That we associate bathing with privacy so tenaciously may have its roots in the Victorian era. The mechanization of bathing occurred at a time when fear of the human body went hand in hand with a new interest in health, exercise, and physical rejuvenation. The early nineteenth century brought about a renewed interest in the therapeutic value of steam baths, for example, but such therapy took place in segregated cubicles: vapor baths and portable steam baths all adapted the water and heat technology of earlier times to the privacy of the home.

The notion of linking nudity with shame seems like a quaint anachronism today. If anything, we celebrate the human body; exposure is something to aspire to, whether it's in the revealing Lycra we wear or the high value we put on being "open" with our feelings toward one another. We invest such openness with a moral value, equating it with honesty and associating reserve with inhibition. Whereas exposure of the body was once considered shameful, today we are more likely to attach shame to keeping secrets. But we are no closer to communal bathing than the Victorians were, and I suspect it is because the human need for solitude is a tenacious impulse.

Our contemporary creed of openness tends to undervalue privacy: we put a low value on the comforts of being alone. Yet we search out solitude in spite of ourselves, moving armchairs and other objects of comfort into the bathroom, the one room in the house where solitude remains a legitimate pursuit. Framed photographs and flowers, exquisite antiques, gilt mirrors, and assorted other accessories traditionally reserved for the living room furnish the bathroom today, as though it were a mini living room for one.

Philosophers, architects, and other visionaries espouse a return to bathing as social regeneration, suggesting that such a celebration of the communal spirit would benefit society, but until we find some other domestic structure or habit that gives us the privacy we crave, I don't think we are going to go in for communal bathing. In *A Pattern Language* (New York: Oxford University Press, 1977), architect Christopher Alexander encourages communal bathing rooms, suggesting that we become less warlike when we tend to ourselves and our children this way. Alexander approaches architecture and design as a sequence of human and social concerns, rather than as issues of construction and marketability. He notes, then, that bathing gives pleasure to the body and sustenance to the soul—all the more so when shared among family members and friends. He recommends a suite or bathing room within which private realms can be created.

Although well intentioned, Alexander's proposal seems remote from who we are and how we live. An architect I know tells me that it is not uncommon for her to have nine or ten telephone numbers with which to reach her clients—working couples at home, at the office, the cell phone, and at various fax machines. Although we are in the grip of a communications mania, what's interesting to me is that the phone hasn't made it into our bathrooms, yet. (Although several phones are regularly found in hotel bathrooms.) While a lot of other high-tech equipment has been introduced into the bathroom—heated towel racks, steam showers, adjustable massage shower heads—the phone hasn't found a place there. A few years ago, market researchers tried this idea out on us, but we seem to have rejected it, recognizing it as an unwanted intrusion. In fact, bathrooms equipped with telephones are not perceived as a luxury but as a joke, a metaphor for work-obsessed potentates who haven't a clue about how to relax.

But there is more to the bathroom than privacy. There's the running water. Privacy and running water are a beautiful combination. Call them the two essential ingredients for clear thought. All the whirlpools, steam showers, and home spas are just about different ways to deliver running water. Too, the acoustic qualities of hard surfaces in this room, and the aural privacy they create, serve to heighten the sense of solitude that can be experienced there. Add steamy warmth to the mix, and there is something primal in the kind of immersion the bathroom offers. Such a place makes contemplation a realm you can float on, drift across, or plunge into completely.

Not that you really need all the equipment. So far as I know, the most innovative and valuable addition to bathroom design isn't the whirlpool or Jacuzzi, but the vinyl shower curtain imprinted with a map of the world. It's a little tacky, no question about that; its colors are murky, its geographic outlines a little vague. Still, if you recognize that the bathroom is a close cousin to the library, a place for solitude and thought, this imprecise atlas becomes a thing of beauty. You're alone, naked, with the map of the world. If the bathroom is the room in the house where people think, this combination could put you in the realm of revelation.

Garage

If the house is a machine for living, then the garage might reasonably be called a living room for a machine, which is not a bad accomplishment for a room whose appearance in the domestic floor plan was made relatively recently. Its spaciousness—the double-car garage door is now said to constitute about forty percent of the front of most suburban homes—and its opulent fittings—insulated garage doors that open and close soundlessly outfitted with faux-beveled, tinted decorative windows, for example—would suggest the uncomfortable truth that our Range Rovers and Lexuses are better housed today than the residents of many Third World countries.

Indeed, in James Wentling's brief history of the garage in *Designing a Place Called Home: Reordering the Suburbs* (New York: Chapman & Hall, 1995), he records its passage from a separate and detached building with secondary status *behind* the house to a cherished domestic space that is a fully integrated part of the house. In the prewar era, cars tended to be parked in small sheds behind the house, as were the carriages and horses that preceded them. But an attached garage that led directly into the house was quickly perceived to improve the value of the house, and so it became an appendage to the back of the house. But then, homeowners and designers realized that if they moved the garage even further forward to adjoin the side of the house, this new plan would allow for more yard space behind the house. Better yet, it would leave room to build another room behind the garage—yet another building plan that placed the garage in an even more assertive and prominent position in the front of the house.

And as the garage moved forward, it grew as well, its expanding size reflecting both its growing status in the domestic floor plan and the continuing growth of the American automobile. The car park, popular during the forties and fifties as a kind of casual and relatively less expensive shelter for the automobile, was never very popular, probably because, without walls, it always came off as simply an ad hoc arrangement that didn't hold the car in the full esteem it deserved.

Today, of course, the garage is a place that gets full respect. An old adage claims that the average homeowner pays more to house his car than his children. And as Wentling relates, the average one-car garage, about 250 square feet, is twice the size of most secondary bedrooms. Between 1930 and 1960, the automobile went from occupying fifteen percent of the first floor plan to about forty-five percent, in the process dramatically revising the structure and style of the facade of the contemporary home (Virginia and Lee McAlester, *A Field Guide to American Houses*, New York: Alfred A. Knopf, 1984).

That the garage holds such an esteemed position in the contemporary American floor plan is in part due to its function as front door and entry way. Human nature being what it is, people usually will opt to get to their destination using the most direct route. But while the most efficient route into the house may be through the garage door, such a passage nevertheless leans more toward cement flooring and concrete steps rather than any clearly marked walkway or more gracious route.

In *A Pattern Language* (New York: Oxford University Press, 1977), a kind of moral guidebook for architecture, building, and planning, architect Christopher Alexander suggests a different logic, sensibly advocating that the place that connects the car to the house be treated seriously as a beautiful and significant space in its own right, a positive space that "supports the experience of coming and going." Alexander advocates "making a room out of the place for the car," possibly with columns, low walls, the edge of the house, plants, a trellised wall, a place to sit. "A proper car connection," he writes "is a place where people can walk together, lean, say goodbye."

While Alexander's lyrical image of a gracious, plant-filled "room" for the car fully addresses the social and design function of the garage, its revered status in the contemporary home surely has as much to do with its role as sanctuary and shrine to the automobile. Our love affair with cars reflects a complex intersection of American obsessions, including those with machines, money, status, and speed. But certainly it has something to do as well with what Alexander refers to as "the experience of coming and going." Which, of course, is not simply what we all do every day when we go to work, to school, to the store. Coming and going resonates as well with the mythology of travel that holds such a firm place in our cultural imagination.

The lures of the highway, the narrative of the journey, the epic discoveries made on the open road are all essential to the formation of the American character. The image of the outlaw drifter has evolved over the generations from Wild Bill Hickock and Cheyenne Bodie to Jack Kerouack and Hunter Thompson. The itinerant pilgrim, whose outcast status is matched only by his vast reservoir of moral right, has been a cherished American icon and role model for generations of young men especially, Thelma and Louise notwithstanding. Small wonder, then, that the place where the vehicle for these illuminating travels resides has acquired its own celebrated status. It is the departure point for the solitary odyssey, the place where the trite experiences of domesticity are traded in for the adventures of the open road.

Having in one way or another come by the information that domesticity has its comforts and solaces as well as its burdens, most men, of course, don't take flight. Still, the garage remains a place that holds out the *possibilities* of flight. The garage, then, is a marginal, transitional space that can accommodate any number of ad hoc domestic needs. As the kitchen drawer of the house, it usually serves some functional purpose or another. It might be a playroom for the kids, but is more likely to be a utility room or storage space. Most of all it may be that domestic space where men can find solitude. For many families, the garage remains a man's private fiefdom, the only turf he fully controls, with little chance of being tidied and straightened out by any conspiracy of wives, girlfriends, cleaning ladies.

It is exactly this clutter and solitude, the tinkering and fooling around there that most identify the garage workshop as a place of invention, a kind of alternative studio, a laboratory of the ordinary. The Performing Garage, an alternative theater space in New York City, takes its name in part from the innovative work that invariably emerges from this grimy, utilitarian, and clearly de-aestheticized studio. Set constructions might be adapted from one performance to another; implicit in its name is the idea that innovation can come from rethinking, reworking, and reconstructing the ordinary objects and materials that are at hand.

The enduring appeal and value of the American garage was clarified most succinctly to me recently by my friend John Scofield, a designer and sculptor in Kent, Connecticut, who remarked that "If there is anything uniquely American about the way I work, it might be that an inventor doesn't always need Bell Labs behind him to find something of value in the known universe. That's what the garage is for." Scofield oils his shotgun there as though it were a piece of fine art and he assembles sculpture there as though it were a machine to calibrate the unpredictable circumstances of modern experience. The garage is a place where these two lines of work might be understood to be parallel enterprises. The beauty of the place is that it's a democratic studio.

Sometimes our strongest associations with place seem to be derived from a logic all their own. The image of the garage that stays most in my mind is resonant with the future, but not because its a place that promises imagined road trips in which man or woman alike can drive fast and far from the oppressions of domesticity, nor for any mechanical invention that might take shape there. When I was a child, my family briefly resided in a small house in the Sunset district of San Francisco. In 1960, for the Kennedy/Nixon presidential election, our one-car garage was for some reason the designated voting place for the immediate neighborhood. So for that one day, the car was parked on the street, its place taken by a voting booth. Thus occupied by the machinery of choice, perhaps the ultimate accessory of the future, the garage became a place of even greater possibilities. What emerged from that booth that day was, of course, something of value in the known universe. And for that one day, that garage was, in every sense imaginable, a place of coming and going.

Living Room

A woman I know was dating a Hollywood agent. This is not the opening line of a joke; it just sounds like one because the story illustrates the way many people think about design, which, itself, often sounds like a joke. Anyway, he was at her house one evening soon after they met, and he admired the color of her living room walls and a painting on one of them. Then he said, "I should do something like that in my house. But I guess I'll have to get a personality first."

This is a true and wonderful story, because it illustrates precisely the way people often think about design: they think of it as an expression of personality. Part of me loves this confusion because, I suspect, it's behind the decoration of some fantastic and extravagant places. "Expressions," after all, are what you get when you think that design is about personality. What else could possibly explain a foyer door wrapped in white leather and studded with oxidized copper nails, shown recently in a popular decorating magazine?

But I also resent this confusion because I don't think design has much to do with personality, and even less with personal expression. That's style. I think design is more about finding order and comfort in the physical world— whether it is in the arrangement of type on the printed page, furniture in a room, or buildings on a street. Since order and comfort are not easy to come by these days, I find design interesting and, at times, even important. More so than personality, anyway. All of which comes to mind when you consider the living room, the region in the home where design and personality get mixed up the most.

The confusion probably happens because the living room is the most public part of the home, which, by its nature, is a private place. And how we reconcile the privacy of our homes with the public aspect of its spaces says much about how we choose to define ourselves to others. Home is where we can be alone and be ourselves; it is where we dress, cook, eat, bathe, and sleep in what is usually a sequence of personal, private activities. But what we do in the living room may be even more essential to civilized behavior than these everyday activities; in the living room we sit around and talk. Perhaps this is why we call it the *living* room, as though what we do in the other rooms weren't about living.

While sitting around talking may not be done any less now than in earlier times, it was once practiced as a more rigorous discipline. And historically, the places once designed for conversation were more varied and more richly decorated than today. Indeed, what we know as the living room has evolved from a variety of different spaces absent in most contemporary homes. The precedent for the modern living room was, in fact, the parlor found in medieval monasteries, the room where visitors convened to speak with those within the religious order. Hence the name of the room, from the French *parler*. By the late fourteenth century, the parlor had become a part of the house, functioning as an informal receiving area as well as a place to sit or to eat. Later, it was often outfitted as a general receiving area with a bed—for use both by guest and host. Indeed, as the informal, all-purpose living area, the early parlor may be the forbear of the large, open-plan living rooms that became popular some five centuries later.

When people were less likely to search for entertainment elsewhere, different spaces within the house were designed for a variety of social gatherings. In the seventeenth century, the bedroom was the common reception area, although the social tenor of those gatherings may have been more ceremonial that comfortable or relaxing. Toward the end of that century in both England and France, the bed-chamber was often a very public and very formal reception area, with elaborate upholstery and bed-hangings, often complete with the family coat of arms.

By the nineteenth century, however, the domestic interior had vastly adapted to people's need—and desire—for more varied social gatherings. In a time when the acquisition of knowledge was an exalted activity and its exchange part of social discourse, the library, a room set aside for books, became one such meeting place. The dark paneling of walls and shelves conveyed an unmistakably masculine impression, emphasizing that book learning was a man's endeavor. Women received their guests in the more frivolous, feminine drawing room, where the decoration tended to be light, refined, and fashionable.

Too, English manor houses in the mid-1800s revived the use of the Renaissance great hall, a central space often two stories high where large social gatherings for the manor's tenants might be held. Add to such spaces the billiards parlor, the smoking room, and the conservatory, and it is clear that each served different activities around which socializing was organized—assemblies in which cogent conversation played an important part. The variety of environments encouraged, indeed enhanced, the many different ways people could sit around and talk.

If the living room is the social region of the house, it's no surprise that changes in our social habits are reflected in its changing floorplan. Whereas there was once a rigid division between the public and private areas of the house, there is less of a distinction between our public and private lives today. In accordance, we require fewer rooms in the house, and all the various areas once necessary for social gatherings are now often combined into a single space. The formal living room used to receive visitors is becoming a thing of the past, replaced today by something called The Great Room, a kind of all-purpose gathering space, a hybrid of the medieval great hall and the fifties family room. Even with TVs, VCRs, and CD players to entertain us at home, sitting around and talking remains a social activity humans have a natural aptitude for. That gathering space, whatever name it goes by, remains a place that is furnished as much by language as it is by any accommodating arrangement of furniture.

Discussing the plans and furnishings of domestic space in his book *An Illustrated History of Interior Decoration*, historian Mario Praz points to the mid-eighteenth century as the time

when people started to arrange interiors into small and intimate spaces. "These suites assume an air that we might call
coquettish today. Rigid lines, sharp corners were avoided,
on every side there was a smiling curve: the eye followed
the outline of a piece of furniture as if it were a sinuous line
of a woman's body. The armchair embraced the form of the
person who sat in it, and allowed ladies' dresses to be com-
fortably arranged. Thus in decorations, furniture, dress, and
manners, a harmony reigned such as was probably never
seen before (except perhaps in the Italian Renaissance,
though in that case the accent was not chiefly on interior
decoration);. . . and as furniture thus acquired a greater
personality, the artists who depicted it in their paintings and
prints treated pieces of furniture like people, no longer
summarily as mere accessories."

The mid-eighteenth century was not only when we started
to assemble interior spaces in comfortable and humane
arrangements, but it was also when we started to perceive it
in an entirely new way. That is to say, it was when we first
accepted the notion that furniture might be treated as a person. I am of mixed feeling about this—surely it is a fundamentally misguided notion. When you start to treat a piece

of furniture as a person, you are not far off from the assumption that design is about personality. And in fact, a joke going around the design community in the late eighties maintained that designers were simply people who treated objects like women.

Also, it may not be long before you treat a person like a piece of furniture, which is not an entirely uncommon assumption in our social exchanges today. The dope dealers I encountered from time to time in college often referred to their commodity as "furniture dope," assuming it was desirable to smoke stuff that would make you dumb and speechless. Indeed, if Praz talks about eighteenth-century painters treating furniture as people, consider what one reviewer said recently of the characters in Bret Easton Ellis's novel *Glamorama*: "The quasi famous are the furnishings in this novel: They take up space in the same way that armchairs and ottomans and hatstands fill the pages of nineteenth-century fiction."

But all of that said, I would still argue that such confusions do occasionally offer their own rewards. There are times in life when ordinary expectations are reversed and when treating furniture as a person seems the sensible thing to do. Or when you meet up with a piece of furniture that can *only* be treated as a person. This has happened to me just once. When my sister and I were young, we spent our summers visiting our grandparents at their home on Cape Cod, and a good portion of that time was spent in their sprawling living room, a place furnished with a chintz-covered sofa, enormous glass ashtrays, and Reader's Digest condensed books. My grandfather's armchair was the *tour de force* of the room. A nondescript square shape with upholstery the color of dust, it was altogether undistinguished until you made the extraordinary discovery that the chair was mounted on a fully rotational base and could be turned 360 degrees. You could face the other occupants of the room, you could face the landscape of marsh, bay, and sky outside the vast plate glass window next to it, or you could simply face the wall. And for young children, of course, the chair was a constant carnival ride, and we would spend hours spinning one another around on it. Enduring and resilient, patient with our exertions and capable of taking in all views, the chair was the perfect surrogate friend and parent. Clearly this was a chair worth treating as a person.

A friend of mine who is an architect speaks with the same adoring nostalgia of his mother's Swedish Modern coffee table. More than just a place to put your cup or your magazines, the table was a feat of postwar mechanical engineering, designed at a time when even inanimate objects were valued for their ingenuity, capability, and often sublime utility. The table was outfitted with an innovative system of hinged panels; with a few simple maneuverings, it could suddenly be elevated eighteen inches to serve as a dining table, morphing both itself and the function of the room.

There is a certain logic to the fact that both this transformative table and my grandfather's rotating chair resided in the living room, the public, congenial place in the house where even the furniture is apparently capable of having an active presence. And while people who behave as furniture rarely hold out much appeal, there is something invariably engaging about furniture that has its own social life. If such a thing can happen, it might be in this part of the house, a room intended for discourse and social interaction. For it is through conversation and human exchange that known boundaries can be transcended, and in ordinary talk that the unlikely so often transpires.

Epilog

If it is possible to treat a piece of furniture like a person, there are also times when you might reasonably consider treating a house like someone you would listen to. A recent experience put me in mind of this. Last Fall my husband and I received a bill from our gas and electric company, and it was off the charts, more than twice what it should have been for that time of year. Before paying it, we queried the utility company which, in turn, posed to us its own list of questions, everything from whether we had recently bought any new appliances to whether we'd been using any appliances more than before, to whether the kids just tend to leave the refrigerator door open. No, we answered to all.

The utility company then sent a district representative to our house to review our "power use." When she arrived, I led her to the basement (dirt floor), where her disdain for old houses ("God, I love old houses," muttered with a mixture of contempt and frustration) was later tempered by the reluctant admission that she, too, owned such a house. After looking over the circuit breakers and doing her best to inventively deconstruct its totally fictitious record of which appliances were connected to which circuits, she finally located the one that was surging with power almost constantly. "There's your problem," she told me. "Now, what's this connected to?"

I couldn't guess. No, we don't have a waterbed and no, we had not recently installed a jacuzzi. What she did then, was walk through the house, room by room, listening. She walked silently through kitchen, living room, dining room, bedrooms, and bath, pausing in each, cocking her head to hear whatever faint sound there might be of a rogue household appliance or mechanism gone awry, running permanently and errantly, be it the subtle vibrations of the refrigerator, the motor of the water pump, the fan of the convection oven. A friend of mine who is an actor speaks with irony about having to discern the differences between the silences and pauses in the work of Harold Pinter, and it was with that same sense of discrimination that the utility representative listened to each room in our house. She listened to a soundless wall clock, to a silent television, to a hushed stereo. And eventually, when we went outdoors, she lay down on the ground to listen to the faint humming of the underground pump in the septic system, which indeed had gotten caught on a twig, and was running constantly.

Since then, I've been unable to dispel the image of this house as a place one can listen to. In part, that may be due to the charm, delight, and other inescapable rewards garnered when one considers domestic appliances as characters in a Pinter play: Surely it is possible that all their subtle sounds and hesitations are spelling out some banal domestic intrigue of their own. But there is more to it than this. While I reject categorically the idea that my house (or any other) has a personality, I have come to realize that it does have a language of its own, one that includes not only the slight sounds, hums, and vibrations of all the electrical appliances that keep it going, but a host of other interior systems, a network of social and cultural currents, those habits, beliefs, and values that also make it function. And I realize, too, that it is by being attuned to all these systems that we might arrive at some genuine understanding of what it is that gives power to the places we live.